CONTENTS

PREVENTING THE ENTRY OF TERRORISTS INTO THE UNITED STATES

HEARING

BEFORE THE

SUBCOMMITTEE ON
INTERNATIONAL TERRORISM, NONPROLIFERATION
AND HUMAN RIGHTS

OF THE

COMMITTEE ON
INTERNATIONAL RELATIONS
HOUSE OF REPRESENTATIVES

ONE HUNDRED EIGHTH CONGRESS

SECOND SESSION

FEBRUARY 13, 2004

Serial No. 108–90

Printed for the use of the Committee on International Relations

Available via the World Wide Web: http://www.house.gov/international_relations

U.S. GOVERNMENT PRINTING OFFICE

91–797PDF WASHINGTON : 2004

For sale by the Superintendent of Documents, U.S. Government Printing Office
Internet: bookstore.gpo.gov Phone: toll free (866) 512–1800; DC area (202) 512–1800
Fax: (202) 512–2250 Mail: Stop SSOP, Washington, DC 20402–0001

COMMITTEE ON INTERNATIONAL RELATIONS

HENRY J. HYDE, Illinois, *Chairman*

JAMES A. LEACH, Iowa
DOUG BEREUTER, Nebraska
CHRISTOPHER H. SMITH, New Jersey, *Vice Chairman*
DAN BURTON, Indiana
ELTON GALLEGLY, California
ILEANA ROS-LEHTINEN, Florida
CASS BALLENGER, North Carolina
DANA ROHRABACHER, California
EDWARD R. ROYCE, California
PETER T. KING, New York
STEVE CHABOT, Ohio
AMO HOUGHTON, New York
JOHN M. McHUGH, New York
ROY BLUNT, Missouri
THOMAS G. TANCREDO, Colorado
RON PAUL, Texas
NICK SMITH, Michigan
JOSEPH R. PITTS, Pennsylvania
JEFF FLAKE, Arizona
JO ANN DAVIS, Virginia
MARK GREEN, Wisconsin
JERRY WELLER, Illinois
MIKE PENCE, Indiana
THADDEUS G. McCOTTER, Michigan
KATHERINE HARRIS, Florida

TOM LANTOS, California
HOWARD L. BERMAN, California
GARY L. ACKERMAN, New York
ENI F.H. FALEOMAVAEGA, American Samoa
DONALD M. PAYNE, New Jersey
ROBERT MENENDEZ, New Jersey
SHERROD BROWN, Ohio
BRAD SHERMAN, California
ROBERT WEXLER, Florida
ELIOT L. ENGEL, New York
WILLIAM D. DELAHUNT, Massachusetts
GREGORY W. MEEKS, New York
BARBARA LEE, California
JOSEPH CROWLEY, New York
JOSEPH M. HOEFFEL, Pennsylvania
EARL BLUMENAUER, Oregon
SHELLEY BERKLEY, Nevada
GRACE F. NAPOLITANO, California
ADAM B. SCHIFF, California
DIANE E. WATSON, California
ADAM SMITH, Washington
BETTY McCOLLUM, Minnesota
CHRIS BELL, Texas

THOMAS E. MOONEY, SR., *Staff Director/General Counsel*
ROBERT R. KING, *Democratic Staff Director*

SUBCOMMITTEE ON INTERNATIONAL TERRORISM, NONPROLIFERATION AND HUMAN RIGHTS

ELTON GALLEGLY, California, *Chairman*

CHRISTOPHER H. SMITH, New Jersey
DANA ROHRABACHER, California
PETER T. KING, New York
JOSEPH R. PITTS, Pennsylvania
MARK GREEN, Wisconsin
CASS BALLENGER, North Carolina
THOMAS G. TANCREDO, Colorado
NICK SMITH, Michigan
MIKE PENCE, Indiana

BRAD SHERMAN, California
JOSEPH CROWLEY, New York
SHELLEY BERKLEY, Nevada
GRACE NAPOLITANO, California
ADAM B. SCHIFF, California
DIANE E. WATSON, California
CHRIS BELL, Texas
BETTY McCOLLUM, Minnesota

RICHARD MEREU, *Subcommittee Staff Director*
DONALD MACDONALD, *Democratic Professional Staff Member*
RENEE AUSTELL, *Professional Staff Member*
JOSEPH WINDREM, *Staff Associate*

PREVENTING THE ENTRY OF TERRORISTS INTO THE UNITED STATES

FRIDAY, FEBRUARY 13, 2004

HOUSE OF REPRESENTATIVES,
SUBCOMMITTEE ON INTERNATIONAL TERRORISM,
NONPROLIFERATION AND HUMAN RIGHTS,
COMMITTEE ON INTERNATIONAL RELATIONS,
Washington, DC.

The Subcommittee met, pursuant to call, at 10 o'clock a.m., in the Samuel Greenberg Board Room, Administration Building, Los Angeles International Airport, Los Angeles, California, Hon. Elton Gallegly (Chairman of the Subcommittee) presiding.

Mr. GALLEGLY. Today the Subcommitee on International Terrorism, Nonproliferation and Human Rights, holds its first hearing outside of Washington, DC. We came to Los Angeles International Airport to investigate how well our Government is doing to ensure that terrorists and potential terrorists are stopped from entering the United States.

In response to the attacks of September 11, 2001, the U.S. Government has undertaken military actions overseas, increased the tools available for law enforcement and enhanced security at airports. These are all important steps, but the most critical tool we have to prevent another attack is strengthening our immigration system. Simply put, the current terrorist threat comes almost entirely from individuals entering from abroad.

As a review of the events leading up to 9/11 attacks and other terrorist attacks demonstrate, the critical factors to prevent future attacks on U.S. soil are:

The strict enforcement of U.S. immigration laws;

Rigorous screening of visa applicants at our overseas consulates;

Access to databases containing all available information on terrorists; and

The sharing of that information among Government agencies.

A preliminary report by the commission investigating the 9/11 attacks disclosed that as many as eight of the hijackers carried passports that "showed evidence of fraudulent manipulation." Another five passports had "suspicious indicators."

In addition, the panel found that at least six hijackers, including their leader Mohammed Atta, violated U.S. immigration laws. Finally, the commission concluded that none of the hijackers filled out their visa application forms correctly and three outright lied on their visa forms.

Previous reports revealing that the CIA knew that two of the hijackers had al-Qaeda connections as early as January 2001. But that information was not shared with other Government agencies until August 21, 2001. At this point after they had entered our country the two hijackers were placed on the watch list used by the State Department and INS. This was the first missed opportunity.

The second missed opportunity was that this information was not passed along to the Federal Aviation Administration (FAA), which at the time maintained their own no-fly watch list. A General Accounting Office report released in April of last year found that nine Federal agencies maintained 12 separate watch lists. I know considerable progress has been made since the GAO report was issued, but it is my understanding that the Federal Government still does not have a single comprehensive up-to-date list of terrorists or suspected terrorists.

Lax enforcement of immigration laws was not unique to the September 11th attacks. The bombing of the World Trade Center in 1993, the plot to bomb New York City landmarks uncovered in 1994, and the plan to detonate a bomb in the New York City subway in 1997 and the millennium plot to bomb Los Angeles International Airport (LAX), where we meet today, all involve persons who should have been denied visas at one of our consulates, stopped at the border, or deported for violating U.S. immigration laws.

I want to stress that many of our consular and immigration officials have done and continue to do an outstanding job screening for terrorists. The September 11 Commission noted that four potential hijackers were prevented from obtaining a visa by consular officers. A fifth person, an al-Qaeda operative named Mohamed al Kahtami, was turned back by an alert immigration officer in Orlando on August 4, 2001. Officials believe that Kahtami was planning to meet with Mohammed Atta at the Orlando Airport on that very day. Commission members speculate that he could have been the missing 20th hijacker. Kahtami was later apprehended by United States forces in Afghanistan.

However, despite these individual successes and the improvements that have taken place over the past 2 years, it is clear that the Federal authorities need to do much more to prevent terrorists from entering the United States.

I am particularly concerned that our Government still does not have a single, integrated list of suspected terrorists. Further, I will be asking our witnesses whether we now have a policy that clearly states the national security considerations will never again be subordinated to tourism or diplomatic considerations during the entire immigration process.

I do not believe that the pre-9/11 failures resulted primarily from individuals not doing their job at our Embassies or at airports. Instead, I believe we suffered a systemic failure in our entire information sharing, visa screening, and immigration enforcement apparatus. Our Government's number one responsibility is to protect the lives of its citizens. We cannot allow this type of system failure to happen again.

With that, I would like to defer to my good friend from Sherman Oaks, the gentleman who is a Ranking Member of the Committee, Brad Sherman.

[The prepared statement of Mr. Gallegly follows:]

PREPARED STATEMENT OF THE HONORABLE ELTON GALLEGLY, A REPRESENTATIVE IN CONGRESS FROM THE STATE OF CALIFORNIA, AND CHAIRMAN, SUBCOMMITTEE ON INTERNATIONAL TERRORISM, NONPROLIFERATION AND HUMAN RIGHTS

Today, the Subcommittee on International Terrorism, Nonproliferation and Human Rights holds its first hearing outside of Washington D.C. We came to Los Angeles International Airport to investigate how well our government is doing to ensure that terrorists and potential terrorists are stopped from entering the United States.

In response to the attacks of September 11, 2001, the U.S. government has undertaken military actions overseas, increased the tools available for law enforcement and enhanced security at airports. These are all important steps, but the most critical tool we have to prevent another attack is strengthening our immigration system. Simply put, the current terrorist threat comes almost entirely from individuals entering from abroad.

As a review of the events leading up to 9/11 attacks and other terrorist attacks demonstrate, the critical factors to prevent future attacks on U.S. soil are:

- the strict enforcement of U.S. immigration laws;
- rigorous screening of visa applicants at our overseas consulates;
- access to databases containing all available information on terrorists; and,
- the sharing of that information among government agencies.

A preliminary report by the commission investigating the 9/11 attacks disclosed that as many as eight of the hijackers carried passports that "showed evidence of fraudulent manipulation." Another five passports had "suspicious indicators." In addition, the panel found that at least six hijackers, including their leader Mohammed Atta, violated U.S. immigration laws. Finally, the commission concluded that none of the hijackers filled out their visa application forms correctly and three outright lied on their visa forms.

Previous reports revealed that the CIA knew that two of the hijackers had Al Qaeda connections as early as January 2001, but that information was not shared with other government agencies until August 21, 2001. At this point, after they had entered our country, the two hijackers were placed on the watch list used by the State Department and INS. This was the first missed opportunity. The second missed opportunity was that this information was not passed along to the Federal Aviation Administration, which at that time maintained their own "no-fly" watch list. A General Accounting Office report released in April of last year found that 9 federal agencies maintained 12 separate watch lists. I know considerable progress has been made since the GAO report was issued, but it is my understanding that the federal government still does not have a single, comprehensive, up-to-date list of terrorists or suspected terrorists.

Lax enforcement of our immigration laws was not unique to the September 11 attacks. The bombing of World Trade Center in 1993, the plot to bomb New York City landmarks uncovered in 1994, the plan to detonate a bomb in the New York City subway in 1997 and the millennium plot to bomb Los Angeles International Airport, where we meet today, all involved persons who should have been denied visas at one of our consulates, stopped at the border or deported for violating U.S. immigration laws.

I want to stress that many of our consular and immigration officials have done and continue to do an outstanding job screening for terrorists. The September 11 commission noted that four potential hijackers were prevented from obtaining a visa by consular officers. And a fifth person, an Al Qaeda operative named Mohamed al Kahtani, was turned back by an alert immigration inspector in Orlando on August 4, 2001. Officials believe that Kahtani was planning to meet with Mohammed Atta at the Orlando Airport on that day. Commission members speculate that he could have been the missing twentieth hijacker. Kahtani was later apprehended by U.S. forces in Afghanistan.

However, despite these individual successes and the improvements that have taken place over the past two years, it is clear that federal authorities need to do much more to prevent terrorists from entering the United States.

I am particularly concerned that our government still does not have a single, integrated list of suspected terrorists. Further, I will be asking our witnesses whether we now have a policy that clearly states that national security considerations will never again be subordinated to tourism or diplomatic considerations during the entire immigration process.

I do not believe that the pre-9/11 failures resulted primarily from individuals not doing their job at our embassies or at airports. Instead, I believe we suffered a systemic failure in our entire information sharing, visa screening and immigration enforcement apparatus.

Our government's number one responsibility is to protect the lives of its citizens. We cannot allow this type of system-wide failure to happen again.

I would now like to recognize the ranking member on the subcommittee, Congressman Sherman, for the purposes of an opening statement.

Mr. SHERMAN. Thank you, Chairman Gallegly for holding these important hearings. I commend your leadership in bringing our witnesses here today and glad to hold hearings for the entire country here at LAX with my neighbor from Ventura County.

This optic deserves our attention. As some observers may be asking why is it that the International Relations Committee is hold these hearings, it is because we retained jurisdiction over the State Department's visa processing.

Screening applicants who seek to enter the United States is a critical task and begins with the visa process. All 19 of the September 11th terrorists had visas to enter the United States. They all received, from a U.S. consular official abroad, the initial permission to enter the country. Something went terribly wrong when those visas were issued, but the mistakes did not end there.

No one could have known whether or not those 19, or thousands others like them, actually used the visas that they were issued to enter the United States. At the time no one was required to collect or keep track of who used their visa to come here. Had they overstayed their visa, no one would have known. There is to this day no tracking of exit information for the many thousands who visit the United States, notwithstanding the facts that Congress has mandated that work be done.

This is about to change hopefully but the Department of Homeland Security is already well behind statutory deadlines for processing and tracking exits at airports. Only one airport in this county, BWI, even tracks exists and they do so at unmanned kiosks where the visitor just, if they chose to, swipes their card or not so the system is voluntary for all intents and purposes. I want to hear from DHS today how they intend to fix these obvious problems and get the system, known as US–VISIT, up and running at all airports and ports as soon as possible.

As of September 10th your average consular official processing visas to visit the U.S. was primarily concerned with INA 214(b) which is the rebuttable presumption in our immigration law that a nonimmigrant visa applicant was actually planning to immigrate until shown otherwise. That meant that the consular official was likely to admit, say, a young Saudi male if that person had economic reasons to return to Saudi Arabia and, hence, no huge economic benefit of staying, or comparative economic benefit of staying in the United States.

Often the consular official would issue a visa without interviewing the applicant, even without checking the validity of his information or rationale for visiting the U.S. On the other hand, these applicants from other countries with similar demographic profiles and with legitimate verifiable reasons to enter the U.S. were put through the ringer and often cannot overcome the 214(b) presumption. This bias may or may not have been unfair to some applicants, but it certainly was deadly inaccurate.

I want to hear from the State Department witness today what steps the Department has taken to ensure that front-line officers are given the tools they need to interview effectively with terrorism concerns in mind. They need more than databases and criminal background searches. They need to know how to question the applicant in an understanding of the culture from which so many terrorists and attempted terrorists have come.

The State Department has often allowed third parties, basically travel agents, to do much of the processing work, particularly in Saudi Arabia, under the Visa Express program. This was done in countries where we should have heightened security and scrutiny and instead we were seeking efficiency through outsourcing.

In fact, there has been pressure on some front line counselor officials to issue visas to people who did not seem on their face to be 214(b) problems. The first Assistant Secretary of State for Consular Affairs under this Bush Administration was reportedly shown the door because she was too enamored with the Visa Express and similar programs.

She was imbued with a diplomatic culture that saw regular visa denials not as protections of the United States but rather as problems for our bi-lateral relations. We need to maintain good relations with our friendly countries around the world but we need to protect the American people.

What of inter-agency coordination? Of course, it is not the State Department officers that greet visitors when they come here to LAX or other points of entry, but rather DHS officials. We have heard the horror stories about the nine agencies that administered 12 separate lists of terrorist suspects, and lack standardized spelling for translation of foreign names.

It would seem inconceivable that the State Department would suspect someone as a terrorist, but that other agencies, including what was then called the INS, would not know that. While I believe that progress has been made in this area, there is still information that needs to be shared across agencies on a timely basis.

We found that more than 200 visas were revoked in the aftermath of September 11th because of security concerns, but communication between the State Department, law enforcement and immigration officials have remained ineffective. In some instances no action was taken to ensure that suspected terrorists, whose visas were revoked, were not actually in the United States perhaps planning terrorism. I look forward to these hearings to know how the situation has improved and how we can improve it further.

And so we use our oversight function to look at whether the agencies responsible for controlling access to our country are working effectively with the State Department. We need to ensure that information flows quickly to the right people while preserving privacy. Therefore, I look forward to the testimony of the two other Federal agencies present today. I believe that is the FBI and, of course, the Bureau of Customs and Border Protection.

I want to thank the Chairman and his staff for inviting someone associated with Steven Emerson's Investigative Project here today. As you know, this project was a decade ahead of its time in focusing on the terrorist threat to the United States and to our homeland from Islamic extremists so I especially look forward to looking at Bill West's testimony, both hearing it and reading it.

I realize this statement has gone on a little longer than Chairman would prefer and so I will make a few more comments at the beginning of my questioning of the first panel.

[The prepared statement of Mr. Sherman follows:]

PREPARED STATEMENT OF THE HONORABLE BRAD SHERMAN, A REPRESENTATIVE IN CONGRESS FROM THE STATE OF CALIFORNIA

I want to thank Chairman Gallegly for holding these important hearings today. I commend his leadership in bringing our witnesses here to Los Angeles, and I am always happy to hold hearings with my neighbor from Ventura County, be they in Washington or closer to home.

This topic deserves our attention. As some observers may be asking themselves why this subcommittee is here today dealing with this issue, it is important to point out that the International Relations Committee retains jurisdiction over the State Department's visa processing. Notwithstanding the jurisdictional and organizational changes in this area of policy, we on the House International Relations Committee still have a role to play.

Screening applicants who seek to enter the United States is a critical task—and it begins with the visa process. All 19 of the September 11th terrorists had visas to enter the United States. They all received, from a US consular official abroad, the initial permission to enter the country.

Something went wrong when those visas were issued, but the mistakes did not end there.

Nobody could have known whether or not those 19, or thousands others like them, actually entered the US on their visas. At that time, no one was required to collect or keep track of that information. Had they overstayed their visas, nobody could have been sure. There is, to this day, no tracking of exit information for many of those who visit the US, notwithstanding a clear statutory mandate to do so.

That is about to change—hopefully. But the Department of Homeland Security is already well behind statutory deadlines for processing and tracking exits at airports. Only one airport in the entire country tracks exits, and they do so via unmanned kiosks. The system is voluntary, therefore, for all intents and purposes. I want to hear from DHS today how they intend to fix these obvious problems and get the system, known as US–VISIT, up and running at all ports as soon as possible.

On September 10, 2001, your average consular official processing visas to visit the US was primarily concerned with something known as "INA 214(b)," the rebuttable presumption in our immigration law that a nonimmigrant visa applicant was going to immigrate to the United States. This meant the consular official was very likely to admit say, a young, male Saudi citizen. Often the consular official would issue a visa without even interviewing him, without even checking the validity of his information or rationale for visiting the US. Saudis did not often end up as illegal immigrants.

On the other hand, visa applicants from other countries with otherwise similar demographic profiles, with legitimate and verifiable reasons to visit the US, were and are still put through a veritable ringer and often simply cannot overcome 214(b)'s strong presumption.

This bias may or may not have been unfair to some applicants, but it was deadly inaccurate in its judgement of the national security risks to the United States. 214(b) is important, but national security is more so.

I want to hear from the State Department witness today what steps the Department has taken to ensure that its front-line officers are given the tools they need to interview effectively with terrorism concerns in mind. They need more than databases and criminal background searches—they need to know how to question an applicant properly regarding terrorist suspicions.

The State Department often allowed third parties—essentially travel agents—to do much of the processing work under the auspices of the "Visa Express" program. This was even done in countries where heightened scrutiny, not outsourcing for efficiency, was called for. It was used extensively in Saudi Arabia.

In fact, there may have been pressure from above on the front line consular officials to issue visas to people who did not seem, *on their face*, to be 214(b) problems. The first Assistant Secretary of State for Consular Affairs under this President Bush was reportedly shown the door because she was too enamored with Visa Express and similar programs. She was imbued with a diplomatic culture that saw regular visa denials as potential problems for bi-lateral relations, not as a sound national security practice.

What of inter-agency coordination? Of course, the State Department does not greet you at immigration and customs here at LAX or other ports of entry to check your travel documents.

We heard the horror stories about the nine agencies that administered 12 separate lists of terrorist suspects, and the lack of standardization for spelling and translation of Arabic, Farsi and other languages. It would seem inconceivable that the State Department would suspect that someone is a terrorist, but that other agencies, including the former INS, would not know. While I believe that progress has been made in this area, there is still information that is not being shared across agencies on a timely basis.

We found out that more than two hundred visas were revoked in the aftermath of September 11th because of security concerns, but communication between the State Department, law enforcement and immigration officials was often ineffective. In some instances, no action was taken to ensure that suspected terrorists, whose visas were revoked, were not actually in the United States on those visas planning acts of terrorism. I look forward to hearing how the situation has improved, and hopefully will continue to improve.

And so we have to use our oversight function to look into whether the other agencies responsible for controlling access to our country are working with the State Department. We need to ensure that information flows freely and quickly, to the right people along efficient lines of communication. Therefore, I look forward to the testimony of the two other federal agencies present today, the FBI and the Bureau of Customs and Border Protection, one of the Homeland Security Department's three successor agencies to the INS.

I also want to thank the Chairman and his staff for inviting someone associated with Steven Emerson's Investigative Project here today. As you may know, Emerson was years ahead of his time in exposing an expansive terrorist presence in the US, and the relative lack of law enforcement attention paid to them. So I especially look forward to the testimony provided by Bill West and thank him for being here today.

I have had a chance to review his written testimony and would second his comments regarding US–VISIT in advance: the exit tracking component of the program, which I believe was needed long ago, will produce a great deal of information. Who will review this information and what will be done with it remain unanswered questions.

These questions lead to the most important one: how much manpower, infrastructure, and resources will this Administration be willing to expend to ensure the system is done right? The exit-tracking component of the system, if it is done properly, will be costly and require large numbers of staff. We will need to staff exit lanes at ports and border crossings where there currently are none. If the system is to work, funds and manpower will have to be dedicated to this effort. I look to hear from the Administration what resources they will seek from Congress to implement this and its other new initiatives.

Again, I thank the Chairman for holding these hearings.

Mr. GALLEGLY. I thank the gentleman from California. I have had a request from the other Members to have a very brief opening statement. We have a commitment to leave this room at 12:15. That means that I am going to have to cut this first panel off unfortunately at 11 o'clock so I would ask my colleagues to try to focus as much as we can on the witnesses and save our personal comments or make them as limited as possible. With that, I would defer to the gentleman from Orange County, Mr. Royce.

Mr. ROYCE. Thank you, Mr. Chairman. I think, Chairman, if we just focused for a moment on a little bit of the attention to detail in the forms being filled out by those who had a role in 9/11 it would give those here today some understanding of the culture that we face and some of the challenges.

If we went through Abdulaziz Alomari's form itself in which he attempted to obtain a visa to get into the United States, we notice that he claimed to be a student. He does not put down where he is a student. He claims to be married, he is not. He does not put down the wife's name. Claims to have an address but only puts down the hotel in Ryad locally.

Claims that when he comes to the United States he is going to have a location here but, again, cannot provide it. He can provide no proof that he is going to be able to self-finance as he is required to by law. Leaves blank the question of nationality in the form. Apparently leaves all of these answers blank because he just assumes that anyone who fills out one of these requests despite the fact that every one of these answers should have red flagged the visa application.

He just presumes that because he is submitted the application it is going to be approved. Certainly it was and 3 months later we find him with his friend Mohammed Atta smashing a plane into the American Airlines flight 11 into the north tower of the World Trade Center building.

The point I wanted to make in this opening statement is the point that Joel Aubrey makes in an article he submitted in *National View* looking at these 15 cases that they examined. We have some of the former consular officials here who are going to give testimony later. None of these should have been approved and the point he makes is that the intelligence community's inability to connect the dots might not have been fatal had the State Department followed the law and prevented the dots from being here in the country in the first place.

I think the point is that we should now hope that our visa policy will be accorded the same level of attention that Congress is presently giving our intelligence failures. That is the focus of our Chairman here today and we as Members of the Committee have that charge so we very much appreciate the witnesses who are with us today.

Looking immediately after 9/11, as I know you did, Chairman Gallegly, and seeing that some 6 months after that the 2 percent refusal rate in the Ryad office had, indeed, gone up to 3 percent but that is still questionable in an environment where 25 percent nationwide are, in fact, nationwide refused. There is still that question about why the law is not being applied there.

Again, Chairman, thank you for the opportunity to say a few words.

Mr. GALLEGLY. Thank you, Ed, and thanks for being as brief as possible. Keep an eye up there. We have a little light system on.

Tom Tancredo made his way down from Colorado this morning. Welcome, Tom. Do you have a brief opening statement?

Mr. TANCREDO. Thank you. Only to say thank you to the Chairman for allowing me to participate in the event today. I really look forward to this and have been looking forward to it since I first was made aware of it. Nothing more than that.

Mr. GALLEGLY. Thank you, Tom.

The gentleman from Huntington Beach. Is that official, Dana, or do you prefer to be recognized from——

Mr. ROHRABACHER. I guess it is Los Angeles and Orange County.

Mr. GALLEGLY. Los Angeles and Orange County, long-time Member of the Committee, Dana Rohrabacher.

Mr. ROHRABACHER. I will be very brief, Mr. Chairman. First of all, I want to thank you and I think everyone here should thank you for holding this hearing and to focus on something that is vital to the safety of our families and the future of our state and our country.

Let me just note that there is an interrelationship between illegal immigration and the type of security and safety threats that we are talking about when we talk about terrorism. We have a situation where illegal immigration is out of control and it is not just affecting our education system and our health care and our judicial system, but it is also affecting our national security and the safety of our people because of the terrorist element.

I would hope that today we are able to connect the dots between illegal immigration and terrorism. I was just at a forum in Long Beach and a gentleman said,

> "Well, it has everything to do with Mexico. Illegal immigration has everything to do with Mexico and everything to do with Incente Fox and our southern border and I had to correct it."

The bottom line is the stereotype that all of these issues have to deal with just securing the southern border are wrong.

If we are going to make our country safe, we have to deal with the illegal immigration problem and a large part of that problem comes right through this airport. I am here to see if we can shed some light on that and if I can learn something and whether we can talk to the people on hand. Thank you.

Mr. GALLEGLY. Thank you, Dana.

We are very fortunate to have three very distinguished people on our first panel. I want to thank you all for making the trek in this morning. I would like to introduce them and then we will give each one of them an opportunity to have an opening statement and then we will go to our panel.

First of all, I would like to welcome Mr. Robert Garrity. Mr. Garrity serves as Inspector Deputy Assistant Director of the Records Management Division of the FBI. In 2001 he was selected into the FBI senior executive service at the rank of inspector.

Mr. Garrity entered duty with the FBI in 1976 and has worked in counterintelligence, criminal investigations, and information security. He holds a Bachelors Degree from the University of Maryland and an MPA from the University of Southern California.

Our next witness is Ms. Ana Hinojosa, the Port Director, Los Angeles International Airport for Customs and Border Protection which is part of the Department of Homeland Security. In this position Ms. Hinojosa has been responsible for——

I would really ask everyone if you do have a cell phone if you would please turn it off and I will make sure that mine is turned off. Please help us with that.

In this position, Ms. Hinojosa has been responsible for customs, immigration, and agricultural inspections. In addition to LAX, Ms. Hinojosa has jurisdiction over the airports of Ontario, Burbank, Long Beach, Palm Springs, and Las Vegas. Part of this appoint she served as the Assistant Director of Operations for the Southern Texas Customs Management Center where she maintained operational oversight of the Texas border ports from Brownsville to Del Rio and the San Antonio and Austin airports.

Director Hinojosa is a graduate of Texas A&M International University and has completed leadership programs through U.S. Customs and the Columbia University School of Business.

Our third witness is the Consul General at the U.S. Consulate in Tijuana, Mexico, Mr. David Stewart. Prior to his current assignment Mr. Stewart was a member of the State Department Senior Seminar and served as a Deputy Chief of Mission and Charge d'Affaires at the U.S. Embassy in Trinidad and Tobago.

Mr. Stewart has served assignments in Germany, Romania, the Bahamas, and Pakistan. He is a graduate of Harvard University and has graduate degrees from Duke and the National Defense University. You can see we actually have very qualified folks here this morning.

With that, I would welcome Mr. Garrity for an opening statement.

STATEMENT OF ROBERT GARRITY, DEPUTY ASSISTANT DIRECTOR, RECORDS MANAGEMENT DIVISION, FEDERAL BUREAU OF INVESTIGATION

Mr. GARRITY. Thank you, Mr. Chairman and Members of the Committee. Director Mueller could not be here today but he is very interested in this topic and I will be speaking in his stead. I am the Deputy Assistant Director of one of the FBI's newest divisions, the Records Management Division (RMD). I want to talk to you today about two things, the National Name Check Program, where we check the names of those who apply for visas, and also, as the Committee has requested, to talk about the Terrorist Screening Center (TSC) which the FBI administers for our colleagues.

FBI Name Check Program requires the FBI to check certain visa applications that require interagency vetting prior to approval by the Department of State. The primary category is designated Visas Condor, relevant to certain individuals who are from designated countries and who satisfy additional criteria which may make them worthy of additional scrutiny.

The FBI receives information on the applicants from the Department of State, which is entered into the FBI's National Name Check Program (NNCP). The information is searched against the FBI's Universal Indices (UNI). The searches seek all instances of the individual's name and approximate date of birth, whether a main file name or reference.

By way of explanation, a main file name is that of an individual who is the subject of an FBI investigation, whereas a reference might be anytime that name was indexed into our files. It might be a victim; it might be an associate; or it might be some other type of reference to the individual.

The names are searched in a multitude of combinations, switching the order of first, last, middle names, as well as combinations with just the first and last, first and middle, and so on. It also searches different phonetic spelling variations of the names, which is especially important, considering that many names in our indices have been transliterated from a language other than English.

If there is a match with a name in an FBI record, it is designated as a "Hit" meaning that the system has stopped on a possible match with the name being checked, but now a human being must review the file or indices entry to further refine the "Hit" on names. If the search comes up with a name and birth date match, it is designated an "Ident." An "Ident" is usually easier to resolve.

Approximately 85 percent of name checks are electronically returned as having "No Record" within 72 hours. A "No Record" indicates that the FBI's Central Records System contains no identifiable information regarding this individual. By agreement with the Department of State, partially due to our concern about the time factors in approving most visa requests, a "No Record" equates to a "No Objection."

If we have nothing on the individual, the State Department is given the green light that we have no objection to them issuing a visa to an individual. If we do get a Hit, if we do get an Ident, the Records Management Division surrenders that file and the information we have gleaned to one of the four substantive divisions, either the Counterterrorism Division, the Counterintelligence Division, the Cyber Division, or the Criminal Investigative Division for their experts to go through the file and they then reach a decision as to whether or not this individual represents a threat to the National Security of the United States and the FBI may seek to enter a security advisory opinion.

Roughly 1 percent of all the names we receive result in the FBI going back and finding something that might be of concern to us. It does not mean that 1 percent of the names are objected to. It means that in 1 percent of the cases we find something that we have to dig into our files and conduct a review of whether or not the individual is of interest to us.

To give the Committee some reference of the workload that involves, before September 11, 2001, we processed approximately 2.5 million name checks a year. Last year we conducted 8.1 million name checks in a year. The work has increased exponentially and that is why in some instances there have been delays.

I have testified before other Committees of Congress, usually not for the purpose this Committee is looking at. It is usually, "Why is the FBI slowing down students coming into our country? Why is the FBI slowing down tourism? Why is the FBI preventing businessmen from getting visas to the country?" There are several different Committees of the Congress who have an interest in how the FBI is treating names.

The Committee also expressed interest in the Terrorism Screening Center. The Terrorist Screening Center was created to ensure that Government investigators, screeners, agents, and State and local law enforcement officers have ready access to the information and expertise they need in order to respond quickly when a suspected terrorist is screened or stopped.

The TSC will consolidate access to terrorist watch lists from multiple agencies and provide 24/7 operational support for thousands of Federal screeners and State and local law enforcement officers across the country and around the world. When fully operational, the TSC will dramatically increase our ability to ensure that Federal, State, and local officials are working from the same unified, comprehensive set of anti-terrorist information.

The TSC allows for the consolidation of disparate information, currently held by multiple agencies, to be brought together for a single purpose of identifying and detaining potential terrorists, or prevent future terrorist attacks. The creation of the TSC marks a significant step in protecting America's communities and families by detecting, disrupting or preempting terrorist threats.

Since December 1, 2003, TSC has been providing key resources for screeners and law enforcement personnel. These include: A single coordination point for terrorist screening data; a consolidated 24/7 call center for encounter identification assistance; a coordinated law enforcement response to Federal, State and local law enforcement; a formal process for tracking encounters and ensuring feedback is supplied to the appropriate entities.

Since December 1, 2003, the TSC has had the ability to: (1) make the names and identifying information of terrorists (known to or suspected by the U.S. Government) accessible to Federal, State and local law enforcement; (2) systematically review whether a known or suspected terrorist should be included in or deleted from additional screening processes; (3) administer a process to ensure that persons, who may share a name with a known or suspected terrorist, are not unduly inconvenienced in U.S. Government screening processes; and, (4) implement a system to adjust or delete outdated or incorrect information to prevent problems arising from misidentifications.

The nature of the terrorist, foreign intelligence and criminal threats facing our nation continues to evolve and so does the FBI. We have made significant strides toward enhancing our operations, both domestically and overseas, and depend upon valuable partnerships with other law enforcement and intelligence agencies. In addition, the FBI recognizes the importance of accurate and timely name check processing.

I want to assure the Committee that this issue has the full attention of Director Mueller. He has pledged more resources to this issue and has committed the FBI to ensure that we do everything we can possibly do to protect our nation's borders. Thank you, sir.

[The prepared statement of Mr. Garrity follows:]

PREPARED STATEMENT OF ROBERT GARRITY, DEPUTY ASSISTANT DIRECTOR, RECORDS MANAGEMENT DIVISION, FEDERAL BUREAU OF INVESTIGATION

Mr. Chairman and members of the Committee, thank you for inviting Director Mueller here today to testify in this hearing, in which the Committee is examining the FBI's role in the process of preventing the entry of terrorists into the United States. Unfortunately, Director Mueller could not be here today, so I have been designated to provide testimony in his stead. My name is Robert Garrity, and I have served as an FBI Special Agent since 1976. I currently serve as the Deputy Assistant Director of one of the FBI's newest divisions, the Records Management Division (RMD). My goal today is to inform you of two main methods in which the FBI is an integral part of the cooperative effort of federal agencies to screen for potential terrorists attempting to enter this country. The first process is the FBI National Name Check Program which screens selected groups before they receive a visa for entry into the United States. Lastly, I want to provide you with the mission and objectives of the new Terrorist Screening Center (TSC) which assists in the efforts to respond to suspected terrorists screened or stopped at our borders.

FBI NAME CHECK PROCESS

Certain visa applications require substantial interagency vetting prior to approval by the Department of State. The primary category is designated Visa Condor, relevant to certain individuals who are from designated countries and who satisfy additional criteria which may make them worthy of additional scrutiny. The FBI receives information on the applicants from the Department of State, which is entered into the FBI's National Name Check Program (NNCP). The information is searched against the FBI's Universal Indices (UNI). The searches seek all instances of the individual's name and approximate date of birth, whether a main file name or reference. By way of explanation, a main file name is that of an individual who is the subject of an FBI investigation, whereas a reference is someone whose name appears in an FBI investigation. References may be associates, witnesses, co-conspirators, or victims whose name has been indexed for later retrieval. The names are searched in a multitude of combinations, switching the order of first, last, middle names, as well as combinations with just the first and last, first and middle, and so on. It also searches different phonetic spelling variations of the names, which is especially important, considering that many names in our indices have been transliterated from a language other than English.

If there is a match with a name in an FBI record, it is designated as a "Hit", meaning that the system has stopped on a possible match with the name being checked, but now a human being must review the file or indices entry to further refine the "Hit" on names. If the search comes up with a name and birth date match, it is designated an "Ident." An "Ident" is usually easier to resolve.

Approximately 85% of name checks are electronically returned as having "No Record" within 72 hours. A "No Record" indicates that the FBI's Central Records System contains no identifiable information regarding this individual. By agreement with the Department of State, partially due to our concern about the time factors in approving most visa requests, a "No Record" equates to a "No Objection" to the issuance of a visa. The substantive investigative divisions in the FBI, (i.e., the Counterterrorism Division (CTD), the Counterintelligence Division (CD), the Criminal Investigative Division (CID) and the Cyber Division (CyD)) do not review visa requests where there is no record of the individual. Duplicate submissions (i.e., identically spelled names with identical dates of birth submitted within the last 120 days) are not checked, and the duplicate findings are returned to State.

Because a name and birth date are not sufficient to positively correlate the file with an individual, additional review is required. A secondary manual name search usually identifies an additional 10% of the requests as having a "No Record", for a 95% overall "No Record" response rate. This is usually accomplished within a week of the request. The remaining 5% are identified as possibly being the subject of an FBI investigation. The FBI record must now be retrieved and reviewed. If the records were electronically uploaded into the FBI Automated Case Support (ACS) electronic record keeping system, it can be viewed quickly. If not, the relevant information must be retrieved from the existing paper record. Review of this information will determine whether the information is identified with the subject of the request. If not, the request is closed as a "No Record."

The information in the file is reviewed for possible derogatory information. Less than 1% of the requests are identified with an individual with possible derogatory information. These requests are forwarded to the appropriate FBI investigative division for further analysis. If the investigative division determines there is no objection to the visa request, the request is returned to the name check dissemination desk for forwarding to the Department of State. If there is an FBI objection to the visa request, the investigative division will prepare a written Security Advisory Opinion (SAO) and forward it to the Department of State. In reviewing these visa requests, the FBI has identified individuals attempting to enter the United States who are of serious concern to the FBI.

I want to emphasize to you that the FBI is sensitive to the impact that delays in visa processing may have on business, education, tourism, this country's foreign relations, and worldwide perceptions of the United States. With these considerations in mind, the FBI is working diligently with the Department of State toward the common goal of improving the expediency and efficiency of the visa clearance process. At the same time, the consequences of the FBI's mission on homeland security require that our name check process be primarily focused on an accurate and thorough result. This means that there are instances when the FBI's review of a visa request must require as much time as needed to obtain an unequivocally correct result.

PROCESSING TIMES

The FBI's goal is to have all requests completed within 120 days. How long does it take to complete a visa request name check? Ninety-two percent are completed in 30 days. Between 98–99% of the requests are resolved in 120 days. Most name check requests that are over 30 days old are the result of the time required to retrieve and review field office record information. Some delay occurs at substantive analysts' desks, but this is to be expected. These analysts are assigned to the investigative divisions and are primarily assigned to the analysis of intelligence reports from around the world in order to support ongoing investigations, or to support the flow of intelligence to policy makers. Despite these significant and voluminous responsibilities, these are the best professionals to review information in our records, and to then make an informed decision on whether a requester of a visa represents a threat to our homeland, or is interested in illegally acquiring our targeted technology. Nevertheless, as I stated earlier, the FBI resolves between 98–99% of all types of visa requests within 120 days.

DECENTRALIZED RECORD KEEPING SYSTEM

I alluded to the time delay for most requests in excess of 30 days being the time necessary to retrieve the file from the field office where the file is stored. This is the primary factor in any delay in the FBI responding to a visa name check. FBI files are currently stored at one of 265 locations, including FBI Headquarters, all 56 field offices, many of the larger of our 400 resident agencies, several warehouses around the Washington Metropolitan area, in records centers operated either by the National Archives and Records Administration (NARA) or a commercial concern, four large Information Technology Center facilities on the east and west coast, and at Legal Attaché offices worldwide. Delays result from NNCP personnel identifying a file's location and then requesting the file from a field office. Time delays mount as field office staff search file rooms and then fax or ship copies of the needed file or a prepared summary to FBI Headquarters. This process—repeated for many tasks, not only dilutes the FBI's responsiveness, but also limits information sharing—a critical success factor in working counterintelligence and counterterrorism cases.

One possible solution to this problem the FBI is exploring is the establishment of a central records repository where all of our closed paper files could be located, and our active files stored electronically. Our frequently requested closed files could be scanned and uploaded into our electronic record keeping system, so that Agents and analysts worldwide would have instant electronic access to the information they require for their jobs.

TERRORIST SCREENING CENTER

The TSC was created to ensure that government investigators, screeners, agents, and state and local law enforcement officers have ready access to the information and expertise they need in order to respond quickly when a suspected terrorist is screened or stopped. The TSC will consolidate access to terrorist watch lists from multiple agencies and provide 24/7 operational support for thousands of federal screeners and state and local law enforcement officers across the country and around the world. When fully operational, the TSC will dramatically increase our ability to ensure that federal, state, and local officials are working from the same unified, comprehensive set of anti-terrorist information. The TSC allows for the consolidation of disparate information, currently held by multiple agencies to be brought together for a single purpose of identifying and detaining potential terrorists, or prevent future terrorist attacks. The creation of the TSC marks a significant step in protecting America's communities and families by detecting, disrupting or preempting terrorist threats.

Since December 1, 2003, TSC has been providing key resources for screeners and law enforcement personnel. These include:

1. a single coordination point for terrorist screening data;
2. a consolidated 24/7 call center for encounter identification assistance;
3. a coordinated law enforcement response to federal, state and local law enforcement;
4. a formal process for tracking encounters and ensuring feedback is supplied to the appropriate entities.

Since December 1, 2003, the TSC has had the ability to: (1) make the names and identifying information of terrorists (known to or suspected by the U.S. Government) accessible to federal, state and local law enforcement; (2) systematically review whether a known or suspected terrorist should be included in or deleted from additional screening processes; (3) administer a process to ensure that persons, who may share a name with a known or suspected terrorist, are not unduly inconvenienced in U.S. Government screening processes; and, (4) implement a system to adjust or delete outdated or incorrect information to prevent problems arising from misidentifications.

CONCLUSION

The nature of the terrorist, foreign intelligence and criminal threats facing our nation continues to evolve and so does the FBI. We have made significant strides toward enhancing our operations, both domestically and overseas, and depend upon valuable partnerships with other law enforcement and intelligence agencies. In addition, the FBI recognizes the importance of accurate and timely name check processing. I want to emphasize to you, this issue has the full attention of Director Mueller. The FBI appreciates the interest of the Committee in this matter. I am prepared to answer any questions the Committee may have. Thank you.

Mr. GALLEGLY. Thank you, Mr. Garrity.

Our next witness, Ms. Ana Hinojosa, is our Port Director and hostess this morning. Welcome.

I would just ask again if the witnesses would be kind enough to try to keep their opening statement to 5 minutes. Anything that goes beyond that if you want to have an extended opening statement, we will make it a part of the formal record of the hearing in its entirety.

STATEMENT OF ANA HINOJOSA, PORT DIRECTOR, LOS ANGELES INTERNATIONAL AIRPORT, BUREAU OF CUSTOMS AND BORDER PROTECTION, DEPARTMENT OF HOMELAND SECURITY

Ms. HINOJOSA. Good morning, Mr. Chairman and the Subcommittee. My only statement this morning is to thank you for the opportunity to be able to testify before your Committee and I look forward to answering any of your questions after.

[The prepared statement of Ms. Hinojosa follows:]

PREPARED STATEMENT OF ANA HINOJOSA, PORT DIRECTOR, LOS ANGELES INTERNATIONAL AIRPORT, BUREAU OF CUSTOMS AND BORDER PROTECTION, DEPARTMENT OF HOMELAND SECURITY

Chairman Gallegly, thank you for this opportunity to testify today to discuss the Department of Homeland Security's ongoing efforts to prevent the entry of terrorists and potential instruments of terror into the United States. I want to specifically discuss with you today the operations at Los Angeles International Airport (LAX).

US–VISIT

The US–VISIT program represents yet another major milestone in enhancing our nation's security and our efforts to secure America's borders. US–VISIT also is a major step towards bringing integrity back to our immigration and border enforcement systems.

The goals of US–VISIT are to:

Enhance the security of our citizens and visitors.

Here at LAX, in the first month of its implementation, we enrolled almost 160,000 passengers through US–VISIT.

Facilitate legitimate travel and trade.

At LAX wait times have not increased beyond 1 or 2 minutes in processing individual passengers.

Ensure the integrity of the immigration system.

Inherent in the US–VISIT program is its ability, in certain instances, to identify for the CBP officer fraudulent documents or legitimate documents being used improperly.

US–VISIT also allows DHS to identify those visitors who have overstayed their allotted time in the U.S. and will be available to determine the future admissibility of such visitors. Through the use of airline and ship manifests, DHS receives information that allows CBP to track the arrivals, and in certain instances, departures of aliens from U.S. ports of entry. Information received from other DHS databases, such as the Student and Exchange Visitor Information System, or SEVIS, will be used to confirm a visitor's compliance with U.S. immigration laws. In cases where

DHS has entry, but not departure information on certain individuals, CBP will refer such cases to U.S. Immigration and Customs Enforcement for further investigation, and if appropriate, removal proceedings in accordance with applicable immigration laws.

CBP also uses biographic and biometric data to check the identity of the visitor against the data captured by the State Department to ensure that the person entering the country is the same person who received the visa to determine whether a biometric match occurs. The U.S. Customs and Border Protection Officer will either admit the visitor or conduct additional inquiries based on the verification results. These procedures reduce fraud, identity theft, and the risk that terrorists and criminals will enter the U.S. undetected.

PASSPORT AND DOCUMENT FRAUD

Our CBP officers do not rely solely on US–VISIT and other advance passenger information. Our officers are experts in recognizing people and documents that are not as they appear. The types of fraud we encounter at LAX run from passport photo substitution to biographic page alterations. Here at LAX over the past three months we have intercepted 91 fraudulent or altered passports, and identified 52 imposters attempting to use the valid documents of another person.

ADVANCE PASSENGER INFORMATION

Advanced passenger information is critical to CBP's ability to determine which passengers require additional scrutiny or screening prior to their arrival at our ports-of-entry.

Prior to 9/11, we received advanced passenger information on a voluntary basis from airlines. After the terrorist attacks on our country, CBP proposed mandatory airline participation in the Advanced Passenger Information System or "APIS." With the Administration's support, the Aviation and Transportation Security Act enacted by Congress in November 2001 required all airlines flying into the U.S. to provide us with advanced passenger information, the passenger manifest, and personal name and record data. Using this data CBP now is better able to identify individuals posing a potential threat prior to their arrival at U.S. ports of entry.

APIS requires airline personnel to electronically transmit data on every passenger on every aircraft to CBP upon departure from foreign airports.

In conjunction with the new legislative requirement, CBP also upgraded and expanded its systems to ensure that APIS could keep up with the additional workload. APIS is now a real-time system that runs advance passenger information against law enforcement databases on a passenger-by-passenger basis. By the time a plane lands, CBP is able to evaluate who on the aircraft may pose a threat to the U.S. and take appropriate action.

AIRLINE AND OTHER FEDERAL LAW ENFORCEMENT AGENCY COOPERATION

CBP has a very active Carrier Consultant Program (CCP). At LAX we use this program to gain the cooperation of the airlines in identifying any illegal or suspect activity involving their carrier. We provide training to the carriers in everything from security measures to fraudulent document awareness training.

As a result of the carrier consultant program, foreign carriers have made many no-board decisions at the foreign ports, as well as referred many cases involving various types of narcotics and contraband. We believe that by educating the carriers to identify risks and suspicious activities, we are multiplying our efforts in support of our national and economic security.

CONCLUSION

The Bureau of Customs and Border Protection has demonstrated and will continue to demonstrate unwavering commitment to our port security efforts, and we anticipate that working together with our sister agencies under the Department of Homeland Security and throughout the government will further these efforts considerably. Thank you again, Chairman Gallegly, Congressman Sherman and the members of the Subcommittee for this opportunity to testify. I would be happy to answer any questions you may have.

Mr. GALLEGLY. I knew she was going to go over. Thank you very much.

Before we go to Mr. Stewart, I would like to welcome my good friend, the delegate from American Samoa, Mr. Eni Faleomavaega who has made the trip out to be with us today. He is a Member of this Committee and a very special friend. Thank you for being here, Eni.

Mr. FALEOMAVAEGA. Mr. Chairman, my apologies for being a little late. With a name like Faleomavaega they probably wonder if I am related to Mohammed Ahmed. My canoe had a hole in it. That is why I was a little late.

Mr. GALLEGLY. Thank you for being here.

Mr. Stewart

STATEMENT OF DAVID C. STEWART, CONSUL GENERAL, AMERICAN CONSULATE GENERAL, TIJUANA, MEXICO

Mr. STEWART. Thank you, Mr. Chairman, distinguished Members. I am very pleased to be here today with my colleagues from the Department of Homeland Security and the FBI. The Department of State's visa work abroad is a vital element in preventing terrorists and others who seek to do us harm from entering our country.

We have no higher responsibility than the protection of our citizens and safeguarding our country's borders through the visa process, and we are determined to carry out this responsibility in the best and most effective manner possible. Since the horror of September 11, 2001, the Department of State has taken a number of steps to strengthen the integrity of the visa process. This helps secure our borders while welcoming legitimate international visitors. Let me mention three of these steps.

First, information sharing. The consular officers who adjudicate visas abroad are truly our first line of defense. One of the most reliable ways to stop those who intend us harm is to identify them to our consular officers abroad. In this way, Consular Officers push back the borders of the United States to the application of the visa. To do their job they must have the best information available within the U.S. Government on terrorist threats.

The Department of State working with other agencies has made significant improvements to our ability to share information. As a result of this increased collaboration, the consular lookout system through which visa applicant are run now totals almost 18 million records on people ineligible to receive visas. This number is nearly triple what we had prior to September 11.

The majority of the data in the consular lookout system is now derived from the law enforcement and intelligence communities. We reciprocate the data sharing and DHS officers at port of entry now have access to visa records in our consular database. We are also sharing our consular database with the National Targeting Center, a 24/7 operation of Customs and Border Protection in DHS.

We have also joined in the establishment of the Terrorist Screening Center which we just heard about that will integrate terrorist watchlists and serve as the centralized point of contact for U.S. terrorist information. Together with the Terrorist Threat Integration Center we will rely on the TSC to ensure consular officers have access to the information they need to deny visas to those who would do us harm.

The second step we have taken is in biometrics. The Enhanced Border Security and Visa Entry Reform Act of 2002 requires that no later than October 26, 2004, the Secretary of State issue to aliens only visas that use biometric identifiers. The biometric visa program began in September 2003 and currently more than 60 posts are enrolling fingerprints. With our aggressive rollout schedule, the program will be in effect at all visa-adjudicating posts by October 26.

Under the biometric visa program consular officers abroad will enroll the fingerprints of all visa applicants with electronic scanners at the time of the visa interview. These finger prints are then matched against the fingerprint files of DHS's IDENT database. We are currently doing so at three pilot posts and will bring the remaining posts online as quickly as possible.

If the fingerprints match fingerprints provided by the FBI in the IDENT lookout database, no action will be taken until the derogatory information is obtained from the FBI and review for appropriate action.

Once the visa has been issued our nonimmigrant visa system sends the issued visa data, including the visa applicant's photo and the fingerprint identification number, to DHS. When a visa applicant arrives at a port of entry, such as this airport, the US–VISIT system will use the fingerprint identification number to match the visa with the file in IDENT. After connecting those compare that with the traveler. This one-to-one fingerprint comparison ensures that the person presenting the visa at the port of entry is the same person to whom the visa was issued.

Sir, our third and final step that I am mentioning in my opening statement concerns the human factor, the training, the resources, and the staffing of our foreign posts. In our ongoing review of consular operations since September 11 our overriding goal has been to provide consular officers not just the best tools but the best training possible. To that end we added four security counterterrorism sessions since 2001.

These classes deal specifically with counterterrorism information, the consular officer's role in counterterrorism, visa fraud and malfeasance. In order to bring expertise on interviewing and deception-detection to our officers, we collaborated with a contractor to develop a stand-alone 2-day module on analytic interviewing which was introduced to the new curriculum in November 2003. This course is also being taught at all of our consular leadership development courses which we conduct overseas for mid-level and senior officers.

Thanks to Secretary Powell's diplomatic readiness initiative the Department is able to meet its increasing workload with staffing resources. In FY 2004 we are establishing 93 new consular positions. FY 2005 we are requesting 60 additional positions. This will give us the ground troops to staff this first line of defense.

In conclusion, sir, the Department of State is working hand in hand with our colleagues in DHS and throughout the U.S. Government to ensure that we have a system that facilitates legitimate international travelers and denies visas to those who pose a threat to our country.

I want to assure you that the Department of State and the Bureau of Consular Affairs are determined to spare no effort to secure our borders. National security is our top priority, sir. We want consular processes in which the American people can place their confidence and trust. Our continued commitment to ensuring the sanctity and security of our borders and our nation is the number one priority. I am happy to answer any questions you may have. Thank you very much.

[The prepared statement of Mr. Stewart follows:]

PREPARED STATEMENT OF DAVID C. STEWART, CONSUL GENERAL, AMERICAN CONSULATE GENERAL, TIJUANA, MEXICO

I am very pleased to be here today with my colleagues from the Department of Homeland Security and the FBI. The Department of State's visa work abroad is a vital element in preventing terrorists and others who seek to do us harm from entering our country. We have no higher responsibility than the protection of our citizens and safeguarding our country's borders through the visa process, and we are determined to carry out this responsibility in the best and most effective manner possible. Since the horror of September 11, 2001, the Department of State has taken a number of steps to strengthen the integrity of the visa process to assist us in preserving the sanctity of our borders while allowing us to continue welcoming those legitimate international visitors who enrich our society and contribute to our economic well-being.

INFORMATION SHARING

The Consular Officers of the Foreign Service who adjudicate visas at 211 embassies and consulates abroad are truly our first line of defense. To do their job, they must have the best information available within the U.S. government on terrorist threats. I cannot over-emphasize this point: one of the most reliable ways to stop those who intend us harm is to identify them to our consular officers abroad. In this way, Consular Officers push back the borders of the United States to the application of a visa. The Department of State, working with other agencies, has made significant improvements to our ability to share information. As a result of this increased collaboration, the consular lookout system through which visa applicants are run now totals almost 18 million records on people ineligible to receive visas. This number is nearly triple what we had prior to September 11. We also now have more than eight million records from the FBI alone in our system.

The majority of the data in the consular lookout system is now derived from other agencies, particularly from within the law enforcement and intelligence communities. Information sharing, of course, must be reciprocal. We now provide access to the 75 million visa records in our consular database to DHS officers at ports of entry so that they can view the electronic files we have of every visaed passenger entering the United States. This database permits examination of detailed information in near-real time on all visas issued, including the photographs of nonimmigrant visa applicants. We are also sharing our consular database with the National Targeting Center, a 24/7 operation of Customs and Border Protection in DHS.

We have also joined in the establishment of the Terrorist Screening Center (TSC) that will integrate terrorist watchlists and serve as the centralized point of contact for everyone from the police officer on the beat here in the U.S. to the consular officer in the farthest reaches of the globe. Together with the Terrorist Threat Integration Center (TTIC), which will maintain the principal database on known and suspected terrorists in a highly classified form, we will rely on the TSC to ensure consular officers have access to the information they need to deny visas to those who would do us harm. We are proud that these institutions rest on a foundation that the Department of State laid in the form of TIPOFF, a pioneering system in the use of classified information for screening purposes. The TIPOFF database with its approximately 120,000 records, more than double the amount prior to September 11, is now housed at TTIC. TTIC and TSC together will eliminate the stovepiping of terrorist data and provide a more systematic approach to posting lookouts on potential and known terrorists.

BIOMETRICS

The inclusion of biometrics, in addition to the photograph that has always been collected, in international travel documents is an important step in continuing to improve our ability to verify the identity of prospective travelers to the United States. In the process of screening visas and passports domestically and abroad, additional biometrics can serve as a useful adjunct to existing screening processes that identify individuals who might be terrorists, criminals, or other aliens who might represent a security risk to the United States. The Department of State has invested substantial time, money, and effort to implement the additional biometrics and ensure that international visitors are aware of changes to the visa application process and admission procedures in the United States. Our biometric program, in conjunction with DHS's US–VISIT program, will create a seamless, coordinated and interlocking network of border security, which begins with consular offices collecting electronically scanned fingerprints at consular sections abroad and continues with DHS's US–VISIT program at ports of entry and departure.

The Border Security Act requires that no later than October 26, 2004, the Secretary of State issue to aliens only visas that use biometric identifiers. To comply with this requirement with respect to nonimmigrant visas, the State Department began deployment of the Biometric Visa Program on September 22, 2003, at the U.S. Embassy in Brussels, Belgium, and quickly followed suit at the U.S. Consulate General in Frankfurt and Embassies in San Salvador and Guatemala City. I am pleased to report that the program is now operational at over 60 visa-adjudicating posts and with our aggressive rollout schedule, the program will be in effect at all visa-adjudicating posts by October 26 of this year. With regard to immigrant visas, we will start issuing biometric visas in February and have this program operational at all immigrant visa-adjudicating posts by October 26, 2004.

Consular officers abroad oversee the fingerprint enrollment of the visa applicants with fingerprint scanners at the time of the visa interview. Enrollment time averages about 30 seconds. As soon as the fingerprints are enrolled they are sent electronically, along with the photo of the applicant and biographic data, to the Consular Consolidated Database (CCD) in Washington where they are relayed to DHS's IDENT system, which sends the results back to the CCD for relay back to the post. We are currently doing so at three pilot posts and will bring the remaining posts on-line as quickly as possible. No visa can be issued until a response of no derogatory information found is returned from the IDENT system. Until such information from IDENT is received, the visa system is locked with regards to that visa application. If the fingerprints match fingerprints provided by the FBI in the IDENT lookout database, the IDENT system returns to the post an FBI file number.

At present, Consular officers at posts overseas do not have desktop access to the FBI record associated with that file number. As an interim procedure, we are processing such cases through our National Visa Center, where an FBI official receives and analyzes the FBI's records and then forwards the information to post. We are discussing means to enhance the efficiency of the criminal background check process with the FBI, so that consular officers in the field will have more direct access to National Crime Information Center (NCIC) information that will be of use in adjudicating the visa to conclusion.

If there is no match against the IDENT lookout database, the visa applicant's fingerprints are stored in the US–VISIT database in IDENT, and a fingerprint identification number (FIN) is returned to the post. Once the visa has been issued, our nonimmigrant visa system sends to the DHS Interagency Border Inspection System (IBIS) the issued visa data, including the visa applicant's photo and the fingerprint identification number. When the visa applicant arrives at a port of entry, the US–VISIT system will use the fingerprint identification number to match the visa with the file in IDENT, and will compare the visa holder's fingerprints with those on file. This one-to-one fingerprint comparison ensures that the person presenting the visa at the port of entry is the same person to whom the visa was issued.

Since biometric data has only recently begun to be incorporated into the U.S. visa issuing process, we are taking steps to ensure the continued integrity of those visas issued before biometrics were introduced. There are currently some 20 million valid nonimmigrant visas that are not biometric visas. Our visa datashare program has been upgraded for use at primary inspection under US–VISIT, and we are thus able to ensure the integrity of these valid visas that do not have associated biometric data captured at the time of visa issuance. Under visa datashare, the biographic data and photo from the issued nonimmigrant visa are provided electronically to DHS. When the DHS officer scans the visa at primary inspection, the photo and biographic data of the applicant are extracted from the database and projected on the screen. If the traveler has altered the photo on the visa, the DHS officer will be able to make a comparison with the original photo.

VISA PROCEDURAL CHANGES SINCE 9/11

The Bureau of Consular Affairs has undertaken a systematic review of the visa process in the aftermath of September 11 to identify and eliminate vulnerabilities in the system.

Interview—We established a new worldwide standard for visa interview policy. On August 1, 2003, new regulations were implemented which limit the waiver of personal appearance for nonimmigrant visa applicants to only a few categories of exceptions, such as diplomats, children, and the elderly. Interviewing visa applicants is a powerful tool that assists consular officers in making critical visa decisions. There is almost no substitute for a direct, face-to-face exchange between an applicant and a consular officer to help establish an applicant's credibility. This personal evaluation can verify that the individual portrayed in the application is actually the intended visa recipient. This new standard will also support biometric enrollment via fingerprinting, as mandated by Congress.

SAO—We added additional security clearance checks for counter-terrorism purposes for certain groups of applicants. These security clearances are subject to an inter-agency review process by the intelligence and law enforcement communities. We are also investing one million dollars to develop an improved security clearance process that will use our Consular Consolidated Database to improve the electronic sharing and exchange of security-related data among posts, the Department and clearing agencies. This new project will enhance the efficiency of the security clearance process and allow for real-time exchange of data.

Visa Revocations—We have strengthened procedures following revocation of a visa by ensuring timely notice of the revocation to DHS and the FBI and by creating a shared visa revocation lookout code between State and DHS lookout systems. We also started automated cross-checking of new derogatory information concerning terrorists or suspected terrorists (including TIPOFF entries) against records of previously issued visas in order to revoke existing valid visas in the hands of those who may be a threat.

TRAINING, RESOURCES AND STAFFING

The Bureau of Consular Affairs seeks to provide consular officers not just the best tools, but also the best training possible. To this end, we have made major changes in the consular training course. We added four security/Counter-terrorism sessions since 2001. Two of those classes deal specifically with Counter-terrorism information, one of which is run by CIA/CT staff. The other session is a presentation on the consular officer's role in counter-terrorism, presented by the Secretary's Coordinator for Counter-Terrorism. Consular training now includes a third new session run by Diplomatic Security on visa fraud and malfeasance, which includes a piece on how to protect against visa fraud. The fourth "add-on" session is a lecture on how consular officers should use section 212(a)(3)(B)—the terrorism provision of the Immigration and Nationality Act.

Training—In order to bring expertise on interviewing and deception-detection to our students, we contracted with outside interviewing experts to develop training specifically designed to improve the interviewing skills of consular officers. We took training specialists to our Embassies in Cairo and Mexico to see live visa interviews and then brought them to the Foreign Service Institute to see and critique our existing interviewing training. As a result, we collaborated with the contractor to develop a stand-alone, two-day module on analytic interviewing, which was introduced in to the new curriculum in November 2003. In the longer and revised training curriculum, we believe that we are presenting important, useable information on interviewing and counter-terrorism to our students. Our goal is to provide consular officers with expertise and the best tools available as they begin their critical roles in protecting U.S. border security.

But training does not stop with the classroom—it is an on-going process. We have instructed consular chiefs abroad to develop follow-up training programs and briefings for new consular officers. We are also updating the skills of experienced consular officers at numerous opportunities. The interviewing course is also being taught at the many Consular Leadership Development courses which we conduct each year abroad (19 since 9/11) and in the Advanced Consular course here in DC to train our mid and senior level officers as well. The additional training opportunities have been welcomed by consular officers who want to meet the highest professional standards. We have conveyed to consular chiefs and Chiefs of Missions the importance of consular officers in the country team process, especially the interagency terrorist information committee known as Visa Viper, to ensure that they are full players in connecting the dots by sharing information among agencies at posts abroad.

Staffing—Let me say a few words about the people behind the systems. Thanks to Secretary Powell's Diplomatic Readiness Initiative, the Department is able to meet the increasing workload with the staffing resources to address this critical homeland security requirement. In FY 2004, the Department is establishing 93 new consular positions—13 domestic and 80 overseas. And in FY 2005, the Department is requesting 60 additional positions—15 domestic and 45 overseas. In addition to these, we are establishing 68 new positions overseas in FY–04 and requesting 63 in FY–05 as part of the Consular Associate replacement program. These additional positions will give us the ground troops necessary to staff our first line of defense.

CONCLUSION

We are by no means done. We continue to review our current procedures and processes and are actively working on new initiatives to build on what we have already done. This year we will introduce a new tamper-resistant and machine-readable immigrant visa foil to include digitized photo and fingerprints; eliminate additional vulnerabilities in the visa system by requiring all seamen to obtain individual visas; begin review of "rules based process" as a tool for visa screening; expand our pilot programs on facial recognition technology to combat fraud; increase our consular databases capacity to handle additional data from new sources; complete worldwide deployment of biometric visa capability; and continue discussions with the international community to expand data sharing on terrorist and criminal suspects.

The Department of State is working hand in hand with our colleagues within the U.S. Government to ensure that we have a system that continues to facilitate legitimate international travelers and properly identifies those who pose a threat to prevent them from entering our country. I want to assure you that Department of State and the Bureau of Consular Affairs are determined to spare no effort to secure our borders against terrorist and criminal threats and to create consular processes in which the American people can place their confidence and trust. Our continued commitment to ensuring the sanctity and security of our borders and our nation is the number one priority. I am happy to answer any questions you may have. Thank you very much.

Mr. GALLEGLY. Thank you, Mr. Stewart.

Mr. Garrity, prior to 9/11 the FAA was not given the names on the terrorist watch list. Can you tell us if that practice has changed? Can you also tell us whether the FAA is being given this information the very minute that it is made available?

Mr. GARRITY. Prior to September 11 the FBI did not have something called a watch list. That was created during the aftermath of September 11. In fact, one of the things that I did as an inspector at that time, on September 12 I started a 12-hour shift in our 24-hour command post and my job was I was in charge of the watch list in the evening hours for the 12-hour shifts. It was a new creation that we were coming up with to create a watch list to share with FAA. FAA was right outside the door there. We did not have something called a watch list before September 11.

Mr. GALLEGLY. You did not have a watch list but you had an FBI's wanted list. We can go back and discuss things like Resendez Ramirez and so on who was on the FBI's Most Wanted List and was given voluntary deportation on several occasions while he was in the top 10 most wanted list and went on to commit several other murders. Technically I guess it was not a watch list but the FBI's Most Wanted List was a pretty high profile list.

Mr. GARRITY. It certainly was.

Mr. GALLEGLY. The Terrorist Screening Center which will manage a fully integrated terrorist watch list is being headed by the FBI.

Mr. GARRITY. Yes, sir.

Mr. GALLEGLY. Is it currently fully operational?

Mr. GARRITY. It is operational. It has been operational since December 1st. We are still refining the combination of all the watch lists to have one central one. We expect to have that completed by the end of this year. We are doing it incrementally as we are taking in other watch lists. There are 12 different watch lists. We are taking all those watch lists and combining them and making sure that we have one comprehensive watch list and our goal is to have that completed by the end of this year.

Mr. GALLEGLY. Ms. Hinojosa, one of the missed opportunities that we talked about in my opening statement that took place on 9/11 was the fact that although two of the hijackers, Khalid Almihdhar and Nawaf Alhazmi, were placed on the INS Watch List on August 21, 2003. They were not placed on the FAA's no fly list.

As a result, both of these wanted terrorists were able to board airlines on September 11 without being apprehended. Are the airline personnel, both internationally and domestically, trained to use these watch lists so they prevent terrorists from boarding aircrafts either bound for the U.S. or traveling within our country?

Ms. HINOJOSA. Chairman Gallegly, I would like to beg your indulgence. This is my first testimony before a Subcommittee and perhaps I missed an opportunity to provide my testimony. Could I get an opportunity to give you my opening statement?

Mr. GALLEGLY. Your opening statement, as I mentioned before, if it is extended beyond what was given verbally, and without objection will be made a record of the hearing in its entirety. If you have a written presentation, we will welcome it and it will be made a part of the record of the hearing. Was that your question?

Ms. HINOJOSA. My question was whether I would be able to get an opportunity to give you an overview of what I would like to present with regards to what we are doing here at Los Angeles International Airport in support of the Department of Homeland Security.

Mr. GALLEGLY. You mean in written form or verbally now?

Ms. HINOJOSA. I apologize. I am not very familiar with what is the protocol. Do I have an opportunity to give testimony afterwards in the proceedings? I apologize.

Mr. GALLEGLY. Well, what would make more sense at this point since we have started the questioning from procedure would be for you to present that statement. A part of that statement would be answering whatever questions that other Members on the dais would ask. For the sake of continuity now it would be easier if we just add your statement to be made a record of the hearing without objection because we are on a fairly tight time schedule.

Ms. HINOJOSA. Okay. I apologize.

Mr. GALLEGLY. Not a problem. Because of the interest of time. I have been watching my time. It is 4½ minutes. I will defer to my friend and colleague, Mr. Sherman. We will have a chance for a second round.

Mr. SHERMAN. Mr. Stewart, just to put things in context, I am sure that at least 133 visas have been denied to people who just want to come to my district to attend two or three weddings I was aware of. Thousands, millions of visa requests are denied.

Yet, the Congressional Research Service says that the Bureau of Consular Affairs in 2002, they do not have the data for 2003, says that only 133 nonimmigrant applicants were found inadmissible for reasons of security. That is actually a decline from the year 2000 when it was roughly twice that number. I realize you are based on Tijuana which is not a hot bed of anti-American terrorist activity but it just seems amazing that this whole effort to keep terrorists out of our country comes down to denying 133 visas.

Mr. STEWART. Yes, sir. You are quite correct. Most visas are turned down, as was mentioned by one of the Members, under 214(b) of the Immigration and Nationality Act with people that are perceived to be intending immigrants to the United States that do not have a residence abroad and that they will not be returning.

To try to put some perspective on those numbers, our automated systems capture denials based on the grounds of refusal. You are right, the actual grounds of refusal under security or terrorism are quite small. Let me explain how we came to that.

Since 9/11 consular officers have submitted more than 12,000 security advisory opinion requests based on tip-off hits, sort of security terrorist type hits that are in our automated lookout system, the class system that we run all the applications against. So 12,000 cases were flagged by the system and then an American officer writes an advisory opinion which comes back to Washington and gets vetted through the interagency process, law enforcement, and intelligence.

Mr. SHERMAN. This is all made by the numbers hit or not hit with a computer.

Mr. STEWART. Right.

Mr. SHERMAN. So as far as understanding the culture gathering, face-to-face interview, we have taken the human component completely out of it.

Mr. STEWART. No, sir. I believe this 12,000 would include cases——

Mr. SHERMAN. But we do not know how many of those cases were not just the computer deciding.

Mr. STEWART. Right, because the way the records are kept, it is kept on the grounds of ineligibility because it could be that a line of questioning—as I said, sir, the training is helping consular officers develop lines of questioning which might lead to the possibility of being a terrorist. They cannot refuse someone on that grounds but they can write an advisory opinion to get it. Some of those would be from the officers.

Mr. SHERMAN. Mr. Stewart, I would like to hear you more but I have a little bit of time and I want to turn to Mr. Garrity about databases.

The GAO identified 12 databases. The State Department has three. Why do we need 12 different databases? Are these 12 in the same computer formats so that they can be merged?

Mr. GARRITY. The short answer to your question is no, we do not need 12, we need one. That is what we are striving to achieve with the terrorism screening center. We want to take all of those 12 disparate databases which were devised by the various agencies using whatever computer program they wanted to. We are trying to get them all together.

Mr. SHERMAN. If I can interrupt you, I am particularly concerned about the transliteration of names whether they be spelled in Hebrew characters or Chinese characters or Arabic characters. I realize that we have got these old databases that are all screwy. You could have the same name transliterated 12 different ways in 12 different databases. We now have a universal agreement for all Government agencies that when you see a particular series of Hebrew characters you translate that name with exactly the same Latin characters?

Mr. GARRITY. I do not know the answer to that question but I can get back to you on it. I do not know.

Mr. SHERMAN. So we may be adding confusion to our database. Whenever I read the newspaper I see Kadafi's name transliterated three or four different ways.

Mr. GARRITY. We spell Osama Bin Laden's two different ways, some with an "O" and some with a "U."

Mr. SHERMAN. As far as you know, and you are high up in integrating these databases, we do not have an agreed one way to translate those.

Mr. GARRITY. I do not think so.

Mr. SHERMAN. Please do get back on that.

Mr. GARRITY. I will.

Mr. SHERMAN. I would hope that we had already agreed to one way for the entire U.S. Federal Government, for all of our State governments, and that we were working internationally with other nations that use the Latin alphabet so that all Latin-alphabet-using countries transliterate Hebrew or Chinese character names the same way. It is obvious that we are not there.

I would just want to conclude by saying it is amazing to me that an organization that was able to hit the U.S.S Cole, able to hit our East African Embassies, that is killing our troops in Afghanistan and Iraq as only one very tragic but only one successful hit against us here in the United States.

With all the hard work that goes on to these disparate and not yet coordinated agencies, and there are only three of you here. We could have 12 or 15 agencies represented. I do not think that this success since September 11 can be attributed to having everything organized. Instead, we have had some luck.

Mr. GALLEGLY. Thank you, Mr. Sherman.

Mr. Royce.

Mr. ROYCE. Thank you, Mr. Chairman. We have half of the total admissions to the United States last year qualified under the visa waiver program. The visa waiver program visitors are not reported in this U.S. visitor program. I was going to make the observation and ask the question if you take Richard Reed, the shoe bomber who attempted to enter the United States, he came under that visa waiver program. We heard that al-Qaeda is trying to extend and develop further cells in visa waiver program countries, specifically Canada. You hear a lot about Germany and their efforts there.

So, Mr. Garrity, I was going to ask is there any consideration to review the visa waiver program considering that this might be a hole in the system given the intelligence we now have about what al-Qaeda is doing with cells in these particular countries.

Mr. GARRITY. Well, the answer to your question, Mr. Royce, is you are probably correct. My understanding of it, the program is based on one of reciprocity. It is negotiated and it is probably one that the State Department is probably in a far better position to answer than I am. Not to pass the buck but of all the countries in the world I think that we provide visas to those countries who require visas of our citizens and vice versa.

Mr. ROYCE. Mr. Stewart, could you respond?

Mr. STEWART. I welcome talking about that, sir. The State Department takes about 7 million visa cases a year. The visa waiver countries would add 8 million to that so we would be more than doubling our workload. And so as far as if that program were to terminate, we have 900 consular officers. We'd need 630 more. We'd need a lot of facilities. It would mostly be in countries, England, Japan, Italy, our close allies. Especially since the bombings in Africa with construction requirements, security of Government facilities overseas it would take a few years just to have the physical facilities.

As far as what we do to safeguard against people like Mr. Reed coming in through the visa waiver program, the countries on the list are subject to review every 2 years. Prior to the arrival at POEs passenger manifest and biodata are transmitted to the POEs where they run lookout checks on all arriving passengers.

That also can be run through the TSC. Visa waiver program people can be summarily removed from the United States without a hearing so even the source of information that was passed to them, this is talking really about DHS, would not have to be made known to the travelers. Those are some of the built-in protections.

Mr. ROYCE. So I guess one of the questions is if countries like Germany that are a focus, or Canada, if they can reform and refine their intelligence gathering operations internally, that is going to be a very important aspect of this and maybe a consideration in terms of continuation of this program with them because they can then pass on to you the information about certain suspicious cell makers, potential terrorists.

Mr. STEWART. Exactly. The other thing, the law now requires themselves to continue in the program to have a passport with a biometric identifier. The fear is that someone from a terrorist producing country would come in under a false passport so that kind of collaboration is built in the system, sir.

Mr. ROYCE. Thank you, Mr. Chairman.

Mr. GALLEGLY. Thank you, Mr. Royce.

Mr. Tancredo.

Mr. TANCREDO. Thank you, Mr. Chairman. Mr. Stewart, could you help me just to understand the process? We recognize that a huge number of people here, although I think the general assumption made by many people is that all of the people who are in this country illegally simply walked across the border but, of course, that is not true. A huge number of people who are here came by ports of entry with legal visas and passports but simply stayed pass the time that their visa allowed them to.

Could you just help me to understand exactly what happens when that occurs today? I mean, a person is here. They are on a time limited visa. They continue to be here after that. How do you know about it and after you find out about that it has happened, who do you communicate with—with whom do you communicate and what occurs after you get this knowledge?

Mr. STEWART. Well, sir, the State Department works very closely with the Department of Homeland Security on these matters. The people that are outside the United States that come to apply for visas are in our jurisdiction. But once they are admitted or they cross into the United States, then I really want to defer to Homeland Security.

Now, In Mexico we get a lot of people who have been in the United States and they have come back and applied for visas again and we are getting much more information through our class system which would have what you are talking about now, people that have overstayed, people that have been deported, removed. I can state that certainly since 9/11 our consular officers have much more access to the information that Homeland Security would have. We can find out if the people abused their——

Mr. TANCREDO. What I am trying to find out, Mr. Stewart, is what happens here? What happens to the person who is here? I certainly will also ask Mr. Garrity if he can comment. I am just trying to determine how someone becomes aware of the fact, how our officials whether it is Homeland Security, State Department, or anybody else says, "Oh, okay. Fred came in on such and such a date and now he has overstayed the visa." No. 1, do we know about that when it happens? And, No. 2, if we do, what happens after we know about it? Anybody. Help me out here.

Mr. GARRITY. The FBI would only know about it if the Department of Homeland Security notified us or put that person's name in the National Crime Information Center computer, NCIC. That is how we come to learn of somebody who is of interest to law enforcement.

Mr. TANCREDO. To understand what you are saying here, it would only happen that that person would become—their presence here would become known to Homeland Security if that person violated a law, was picked up, and they somehow or the other found out they had overstayed the visa. But there is no way essentially.

What you are saying is there is no way right now of us knowing. A flag does not go up at a certain point in time because, of course, that is part of what we are trying to put in place. Right now nothing happens unless that person gets arrested or somehow gets crosswise with the law and gets his or her name into a database, then that might generate some sort of communication with you.

Mr. GARRITY. As far as the FBI is concerned, yes. Bureau of Border and Custom Enforcement may have some method that they are aware of but the FBI is not aware unless it is in NCIC.

Mr. TANCREDO. Mr. Stewart, once someone—well, this goes to something a little bit beyond the idea of the process at the borders or obtaining a visa. Nonetheless, I have you here for a second from the State Department. The State Department and the Department of Treasury are both pressing very hard for the Administration to essentially get all our departments in the Federal Government to accept the metricula consular as a valid form of identification.

How in the world can you be doing this when you know that the FBI has testified against it and the Congress of the United States has testified to the fact that this presents a significant security problem for them. There is a proposal that has floated. Now it is in the White House, as I understand it, some sort of working group there.

But still the State Department and the Department of the Treasury are pressing for the Federal Government to accept the metricula consular, to get every agency to accept the metricula consular as a valid form of ID. When that form of ID is handed out by another government, of course, we have already arrested people in the United States with dozens of these things, their picture on it, but a whole bunch of names.

It is anything but valid. And considering the kind of security problems that we are having here, I just am astounded, Mr. Stewart, that the Department of State is still pressing for that acceptance on the part of the Federal Government.

Mr. STEWART. Well, sir, all Mexican visa applicants must present a Mexican passport at the time they apply. In terms of the visa process, we are not accepting that card.

Mr. TANCREDO. No, I am well aware of it.

Mr. STEWART. And my guess would be.

Mr. TANCREDO. For the time being.

Mr. STEWART. I think the issue is that when our State Department officials overseas issue documents we expect them to be accepted by the government that would be there.

Mr. TANCREDO. Do our officials overseas give documents out to Americans overseas who they know to be living there illegally in the country of origin—I mean, in the country of residence at the time? Well, you know they don't.

Mr. GALLEGLY. Mr. Tancredo, I know the gentleman from Colorado knows this is an issue I have great passion and concern about but time has expired. Perhaps we can give Mr. Stewart just 30 seconds to respond. If he can give us an explanation for the rationale for why the State Department has embraced this whole concept of using metricula consular as a document for identification purposes when we have no control over the validity of it.

Mr. STEWART. When we issue passports to American citizens abroad, we don't verify their status in that country.

Mr. GALLEGLY. Pardon me, Mr. Stewart. I think the question really had to do more with the philosophy or the rationale for using it as an internal document, not having to do with border control or entering or exiting the country rather than getting into all that.

Mr. STEWART. Sure. Sir, if I could take this as a question for the record and then we will provide you with a little further information.

Mr. GALLEGLY. We will make it part of the record.

Mr. SHERMAN. If I could just comment, there are visitors from all over the world and the United States today. They are buying drinks at the bar here in LAX and proven they are old enough to drink with passports issued by Latvia, Guatemala, Brazil, and I have no reason to think that the metricula consular is any less reliable than a Ukrainian passport.

Mr. TANCREDO. I could give you the information that could help you make that decision.

Mr. SHERMAN. And I will give you information about Ukrainian passports.

Mr. GALLEGLY. Perhaps we should be more restrictive of Ukrainian passports.

Mr. ROHRABACHER. Ukrainian passports would indicate that someone was here legally or illegally.

Mr. GALLEGLY. So does the metricula consular.

Mr. ROHRABACHER. Consular would simply be an identification. Would it not? Thus, someone could use it as identification even if they were in the country illegally unlike a passport.

Mr. Stewart, you talked about our consular officers being the first line of defense and I agree with that. Unfortunately, I think that what is happened, at least in the 10 years that I have been looking at this issue, that our first line of defense has been undermined other than bolstered so often by perhaps people with all the best of motives but perhaps sometimes people who just didn't care. Let me ask you how some of these things affect your ability to determine whether or not someone would be a threat to the United States.

For example, the 241(i) that was a proposal a couple of years ago, can you tell me what the effect of that was?

Mr. STEWART. Well, sir, I was the Chief of the Consular operations in Juarez at that time. You are referring to people that are in the United States and they are out of immigration status allowing them to adjust status in the United States.

Mr. ROHRABACHER. Right. So——

Mr. STEWART. As far as the State Department is concerned, if they are required to go overseas to apply for a visa to reenter, then there is obviously a workload and staffing issue. Again, if Congress chooses to allow them to pay $1,000 or what and to adjust status, that is, again, a DHS issue. Consular officers issue immigrant visas.

People stay in the United States and they are able to adjust status in the United States because the law allows that. Consular officers sense that we have a little more authority overseas because the burden is on the applicant to establish their entitlement to the visa. It is easier for us to turn down a visa overseas.

Mr. ROHRABACHER. Does not our first line of defense have some sort of access to files within those countries that some member of the bureaucracy here may not have?

Mr. STEWART. Well, sir, in some countries that have reliable documents. For instance, we would require a police clearance. In a lot of countries that is determined not to be a very useful document because it can be easily procured. Overseas we speak the language. We know the culture. We lived there so I think we have some benefits, sir, in processing these applications.

Mr. ROHRABACHER. Mr. Chairman, if there is anything that comes out of this hearing, perhaps it should be a message that I am getting already is that there are a lot of things that Congress has done like 245(i) and other things that may be very well motivated. Let us try to get the tourists through in a hurry.

Some of these things have undermined our ability—underlined our first line of defense and then undermined our ability to actually have control on the border and in the war on terrorism which is relatively new since 9/11. Those procedures or changes that were made actually have inhibited us to having that type of control on the border that would prevent some of the terrorists from overseas from coming here.

I do like your designation, first line of defense. I think that is where we have to make sure we bolster our ability in our first line of defense for those people to do their job. Thank you very much.

Mr. GALLEGLY. Mr. Faleomavaega.

Mr. FALEOMAVAEGA. Thank you, Mr. Chairman. I would just like to make a couple of observations before asking some questions of the members of the panel. There is no question that after 9/11 out country was exposed. But, at the same time, I think we have also been the envy of the world because we are such a free nation. Freedom to travel, freedom of expression, religion, privacy.

I think just about everybody outside the United States would love to come and live and obtain citizenship in this country. In my understanding, citizenship in our country is the most sought after in the whole world and I think we ought to be proud of that. Things have changed. The third most populous country in the world, some 486 million people to take care of.

Now we have about 8 to 9 million illegal aliens living here in our country. I think the question now before us, the problems pertaining to the border between Mexico. Just Mexico but Canada as well. I have always been against establishing a new department, Mr. Chairman, because I have always felt that we already have the agencies.

It was just a matter of enforcement. It is a matter of giving these agencies already established the resources to do their job. Now we have 160,000 employees in this new department. We are just adding more problems, in my humble opinion, Mr. Chairman, than what we already have been confronted with.

My question to Mr. Garrity, would you consider the Canadian border more dangerous than the Mexican border because of greater freedom of the people from Canada, free access liberty coming across the border? Here is my follow-up question. Are we applying the same standard now since after 9/11 to those coming from Canada as those coming from Mexico as far as entry visa and everything?

Mr. GARRITY. I can't answer the follow-up question because I do not know and that is not part of the FBI's jurisdiction. The first question, do I consider the Canadian border more or less a security issue than the Mexican border. I know that the threat that was talked about at the millennium, the threat to detonate a device here at LAX, started at the Canadian border.

Apparently there was a belief on someone's part that that border was more porous or there was a higher opportunity for egress into the country than the Mexican border. But I can't tell you that I am in a position of authority to answer your question as to whether or not one border is more or less secure than another.

Mr. FALEOMAVAEGA. Well, in reference to visas I will ask Mr. Stewart. Are we applying the same standard of visa applications and screening as we are going through now to Canada as well as what we are doing now with Mexico?

Mr. STEWART. Well, sir, Canadian citizens don't require a visa to enter the United States the way Mexicans do so that has been an historic difference.

Mr. FALEOMAVAEGA. And they still don't require them? Is that fair? It is the law but is it fair?

Mr. STEWART. Sir, Mexican officials and Mexican people where I live would like to see reciprocity. I think one great difference with the border is we are very advanced in our 30-point smart border accord with Canada. We are pursuing a shared border process. We are working for more information sharing with the Canadians. Our visa policies between the two countries including handling third country nationals are very similar. I think there is a great deal of cooperation across the terrorist security front with Canada.

We are doing similar things with Australia and UK. I think in that way it is somewhat different than where we are with Mexico. We have a 22-point plan with Mexico but we are not as advanced in that. It is also a difference in that Mexico, as you know, borders Central America unlike Canada so the border is quite different, sir.

Mr. FALEOMAVAEGA. I still want to—I think there is something that I always have a sense of respect and admiration for my colleague from Colorado. I think basically his whole philosophy is that if you are an illegal alien, you have got to meet the requirements of the laws before coming to this country. Simple as that. But when you start making exceptions, this is where we get a little fussy and I get to wondering if that really is fair.

My question to Ms. Hinojosa, the top person here in the LAX. How does the LAX airport compare to Chicago and Miami in terms of the operations? Can you share with us what you consider to be the three most difficult problems at this airport as far as security and all that.

Ms. HINOJOSA. Thank you. As far as how Los Angeles International Airport compares to the other airports nationwide, Los Angeles International as far as U.S. Customs and border protection is concerned, we normally measure inbound international passengers to compare volumes. For the last 2 years Los Angeles International Airport has ranked No. 3 in the country with JFK being first, Miami second. Every year our numbers are very close so we are the top three airports in the country. As far as our——

Mr. FALEOMAVAEGA. I know my time is up. What is your number one issue that you are faced with?

Ms. HINOJOSA. I think that U.S. Customs and Border Protection and the Department of Homeland Security has made magnificent strides with the implementation of the U.S. visit program. I think that a good understanding of what the program is and all of the strides that we are moving toward implementing by December 2005 would be a good place to start.

Mr. FALEOMAVAEGA. Thank you. Thank you, Mr. Chairman.

Mr. GALLEGLY. I thank the gentleman from American Samoa.

I want to thank this panel, particularly you, Ms. Hinojosa for providing us this venue this morning. Obviously when we have hearings like this sometimes we go away with more questions than we have answers as a result of the answers we got during the day. Of course, that is a positive thing and that is one of our objectives here today. I appreciate, Mr. Garrity, you being here, Mr. Stewart. With that, we will move on to our next panel.

Our second panel appearing on behalf of the Center of Immigration Studies is Ms. Jessica Vaughan. Ms. Vaughan is a Senior Policy Analyst with the Center for Immigration Studies and is an expert on immigration law and policy and visa programs. Prior to joining the center Ms. Vaughan was a foreign service officer with the U.S. Department and was Chief of Nonimmigrant Visa Section in Trinidad and Tobago. She has a Masters in Government from Georgetown University and a BA from Washington College.

Our next witness is Mr. Peter Nunez. Mr. Nunez was an Assistant U.S. Attorney for the Southern District of California from 1972 until 1982 and then served as a U.S. Attorney for the Southern District from 1982 until 1988. Following his tenure as U.S. Attorney Mr. Nunez became a partner in the San Diego Law firm of Brobeck, Phleger, and Harrison.

Then in 1990 he was appointed the position of Assistant Secretary of the Treasury for enforcement. He served in that position until 1993. Mr. Nunez is currently on the faculty of the Department of Political Science and International Relations at the University of San Diego. He holds a degree from Duke University and is a graduate of the law school at the University of San Diego.

I would also like to welcome Mr. Bill West. Mr. West is a 25-year veteran of the Investigations Division of the Immigration and Naturalization Service. When he retired in May 2003 he was the Chief of the National Security Section for the INS in Miami. In this position he supervised the INS in investigative efforts in counterterrorism, counterespionage, and human rights persecution cases in the State of Florida. Mr. West is currently a consultant for the Investigative Project, a counterterrorism research institute based in Washington, DC.

I also want to welcome Ms. Peggy Sterling. She is the Vice President for Safety, Security and Environmental Issues with American Airlines since 2002. She has also been with American Airlines since 1970. Previously Ms. Sterling was the Vice President in Charge of Operations for America's largest hub in Dallas/Fort Worth.

I would just like to mention also that we had invited a representative from other airlines including United and American was the only one that was responsive and I thank you for being here.

Ms. Vaughan.

STATEMENT OF JESSICA VAUGHAN, SENIOR POLICY ANALYST, CENTER FOR IMMIGRATION STUDIES

Ms. VAUGHAN. Good morning and thank you for the opportunity to testify. This is a summary of my written statement.

Mr. GALLEGLY. The balance of your statement and all the rest of the witnesses will be made a part of the record in their entirety.

Ms. VAUGHAN. Thank you. Terrorists come in all shapes, sizes, and sexes and, therefore, it is unrealistic to expect that even with the best intelligence or the best profiling that we will be able to stay ahead of their plans. The only effective way to prevent the entry of terrorists is to have a layered defense that includes a well-functioning immigration system that deters, detects, and promptly removes anyone who lacks a legitimate purpose for being here.

Such a system requires three things; superior technology, abundant human resources, and the policies to make effective use of both. We have made great strides in harnessing technology to help us in this effort. Programs such as SEVIS, USVISIT, Biometric visas, and information sharing initiatives have dramatically improved our ability to catch known terrorists, criminals, illegal aliens, and made it easier to spot someone assuming a false identity.

As we implement these programs, however, it is important to guard against the tendency to rely on them to do all the work. We have managed to prevent some terrorists from entering but not because their names showed up in databases but because alert officers made good human judgments. Just as a doctor needs to have personal contact with a patient in order to properly diagnose an illness, consular officers and immigration adjudicators need to have meaningful live contact with applicants in order to make good decisions.

It is important to stay the course on this practice and to resist the inevitable pressure to loosen up. Embassy Riyadh, for instance, recently sent a cable to Washington asking for permission to relax the new screening procedures. The cable expressed concern that because of the new procedures Saudis might soon begin to prefer Europe to America and, God forbid, start to eat Nutella instead of peanut butter.

Well, it is obviously important to cultivate good relations. But one would hope that U.S. diplomats would put protecting the safety of Americans before protecting Jiff and Skippy is global market share.

The State Department has done the right thing by reversing its interview by exception policy so that now more applicants must face a consular officer before getting a visa. CIS needs to adapt these standards, too. It is no less important to interview an applicant for change of status inside the United States than it is to interview someone overseas.

Currently many of the adjustors whether through 245(i) or other channels, or sometimes tourists seeking student status have no contact with an immigration officer after leaving the port of entry.

Requiring more interviews naturally requires hiring many more officers to do the work. Yet, at the slow rate the State Department has been hiring, it is still going to take at least 5 years or more before it has enough people to do the job right. This chronic understaffing has led to some serious problems in adjudicating visas overseas. Among them overreliance on the locally hired staff and inadequate antifraud efforts within the consulate.

The size of the consular corps is not the only human resource issue at stake. Equally important is the fact that most consular work is handled by new junior officers on a mandatory consular assignment with limited training and probably no experience in this kind of work.

Most feel no particular calling to consular work and are simply putting up with it on the way to their next assignment. While many do sincerely try to do the best they can, this arrangement is not a recipe for consistently high quality adjudications.

I believe the nation would be far better served if visa work were instead performed by a corps of visa specialists who choose this as a career. Having the best technology and enough staff is important but it is not quite enough. Government agencies and Congress must also avoid adopting policies that undermine successful new security initiatives.

For instance, a new USVISIT system has greatly enhanced our capacity to identify people we need to keep out. Yet, it is going to cover, as you mentioned, fewer than half the number of people who visit the country because most Canadians, Mexicans, and visa waiver program visitors will not be recorded in a USVISIT. Moreover, DHS apparently has no intention of keeping USVISIT its up and running if the lines at the airport should get too long.

In addition to displaying a certain timidity toward letting effective systems work as intended, both of the main immigration agencies tolerate far too much fraud in the system. Part of this is a result of inadequate staffing but mostly it is the result of misplaced priorities.

This is reflected in the lack of meaningful consequences for people who resort to fraud in the application process. Waivers that excuse previous immigration law violations are practically routine. We cannot expect that this laxity toward fraud and deceit will be overlooked by terrorists any more than it is overlooked by the millions of others who wish to come here.

Finally, the biggest policy-related problem that threatens our ability to keep out terrorists is the fact that our immigration benefits programs are outrageously overbooked. For many hears we have been offering immigration benefits to far more people than can possibly be accommodated within the limits of the law. This is the basic problem that underlines all of the others.

BCIS now has a backlog of more than 5 million applications. Not only is this frustrating to applicants and their sponsors but it impedes the effective screening of applicants as officers are pressured to move cases through as quickly as possible.

The Administration sees there is a problem and has asked for funding to address it. Unfortunately, the White House and some in Congress have also suggested adding a new temporary guestworker program that could easily bring in another 6 to 10 million applicants to be dealt with.

The backlogs and waiting lists are not the result of agency incompetence or outmoded management techniques. They are the result of deliberate policy choices: Previous amnesties like IRCA 245(i) and the LIFE Act which brought millions of illegal aliens into the immigration queue and undoubtedly contributed to the increases in illegal immigration over the last decade.

These amnesties have also legalized terrorists making it easier for them to go about their nasty business. No staff increases, no management improvements, no imaginable amount of additional funding could possibly keep up with the crush of applicants that would arrive under the kind of hugh guestworker programs that have been proposed.

One DHS employee recently estimated that it would take 10 years just to do the security background checks on the millions of applicants. Such a program would be as great a threat to our security as any of the other immigration policy weaknesses that we have discussed.

I would be please to take your questions. Thank you.

[The prepared statement of Ms. Vaughan follows:]

PREPARED STATEMENT OF JESSICA VAUGHAN, SENIOR POLICY ANALYST, CENTER FOR IMMIGRATION STUDIES

Introduction. The recent hearing held by the 9/11 Commission on managing risk at the borders has again focused public attention on the important role our immigration system plays in the war on terrorism. Recognizing a terrorist at the border is a lot harder than recognizing some other forms of evil; you're not necessarily going to know it when you see it, despite our best efforts at profiling. Terrorists come in all shapes, sizes, and sexes, and may bear passports from any country. It is unrealistic to expect even the best intelligence agencies to stay ahead of the terrorists' plans. For this reason, the best possible way to prevent the entry of terrorists into the United States is to have a well-functioning immigration system that is set up to deter, detect, and promptly remove those who lack a legitimate purpose for being here. Such a system requires three things: superior technology, abundant human resources, and the policies to make effective use of both.

Technology. We have made great strides in the last two years in harnessing technology to help us identify terrorists, criminals and illegal aliens when they encounter immigration officials. Some of the most successful new programs include:

SEVIS—The student tracking system has performed admirably since its first big test at the beginning of the 2003 school year, despite cries of alarm and outright hostility to the effort from many quarters in higher education. It identified about 200 individuals falsely claiming to be legitmate foreign students, and led to the investigation of a possible smuggling ring.

USVISIT—Early assessments of the first stage of the new non-immigrant visitor tracking project have also been very positive. In its first three weeks, the project nabbed at least 30 wanted criminals, most of whom had successfully escaped detection at the border on numerous earlier occasions.

Biometric visas—The deployment of biometrics in the visa program is going very well. State continues to expand the scope of the Consolidated Consular Database, which includes digital photos and facial recognition technology, helping to minimize the number of false hits and limitations inherent in a name-checking system.

Information sharing among agencies is improving, though it is still incomplete.

These programs have dramatically improved our ability to catch known terrorists, criminals and illegal aliens, and make it easier to spot someone assuming a false identity. But technology-based solutions have their limitations. Systems can crash or slow down to a crawl. Back-up systems are not as comprehensive or up-to-date as the primary system, if they exists. The State Department name-check system used in embassies overseas is at the mercy of the local communications infrastructure, which can be very unreliable. Even in the United States operating speed can be a problem. Observers have reported that the USVISIT download can take minutes rather than seconds, which is far too slow to clear most busy ports at an acceptable speed.

Besides the predictable technical difficulties, there are translation-related problems associated with name-check systems. While they have been improved a great deal since they were first launched, consistent translation of foreign names can be a problem, and the database frequently generates hundreds of hits on common names, which is a source of regular frustration to users. This is one reason why the move to biometrics is so important.

My main concern, however, is not with the technological glitches. I believe these weaknesses eventually can be addressed with improved technology. My real concern is that, since the development of CLASS and other computer-based screening systems, the consular service has become far too reliant on technology to make the decisions, and downgraded the importance of human skills and experience in the process. Former Assistant Secretary Mary Ryan told the 9/11 Commission, that "nearly all [Saudi] refusals were based on known ineligibilities revealed by checking the automated system." This statement suggests that, at least in Saudi Arabia before 9/11, consular officers were not doing their job—that anyone who was not a known terrorist or otherwise listed in CLASS was considered eligible for a visa. This assumption directly contradicts the law, which requires officers to assume applicants are *ineligible* until they demonstrate otherwise. Since 9/11, the folly of this approach, and the importance of the two other ingredients—personnel and policies—has become obvious.

Personnel. We have seen how one alert officer can make a difference: INS inspector Jose Melendez-Perez's decision to send home the suspected 20th 9/11 hijacker; Customs inspector Diana Dean, who pulled over Ahmed Ressam in a car full of explosives intended for the millennium bombing plot; and consular officers in Germany who refused at least three al-Quaeda plotters seeking visas. These officers made good judgments that no software program could have made for them. Just as a doctor needs to have personal contact with the patient in order to properly diagnose an illness, consular officers and BCIS adjudicators need to have meaningful live contact with the majority of applicants in order to make good decisions.

For its part, the State Department last year finally reversed its "interview by exception" policy, so that now a much larger share of applicants must face a consular officer before getting a visa. The BCIS, too, needs to adopt similar standards in its adjudications process. Because we know that terrorist groups have recruited within the United States and that they may send operatives here for lengthy stays, it is no less important to interview applicants for change of status within the United States than it is to interview an overseas applicant. Currently, many of these applicants—often tourists seeking student status, or students seeking permanent residence—have no contact with an immigration officer after leaving the port of entry. This policy is one that made possible 9/11 hijacker Mohammed Atta's posthumous student visa approval.

Naturally, returning to a standard of practice that involves more interviews requires hiring many more officers to do the work. The State Department is very slowly trying to recover from years of hiring fewer new officers than were leaving the service. Last year, there were about seven-hundred consular officers stationed overseas in 211 posts. In addition to adjudicating six million NIV applications and nearly 600,000 immigrant visa applications, they provided a full range of services to American citizens, which can be very time-consuming in places where large numbers of Americans visit and work. This chronic understaffing has led to some serious problems that hamper our efforts to keep out terrorists:

1. At some posts, the workload is so great that officers must conduct visa interviews all day long. In addition to contributing to stress and burn-out, this leaves little time for supplemental investigation outside of the interview, such as document verification, which can be just as critical as the interview itself. Attention to fraud varies widely from post to post, depending on the time available and the priorities of the supervising officers, but more officers would almost certainly boost anti-fraud efforts in general.
2. With staffing so tight, training is often given short shrift, as officers are pushed off to post as quickly as possible, and put straight onto the line. By hiring more officers, the Department would have more flexibility to deal with staffing gaps and training needs.
3. In many posts, particularly the very busy ones, officers are far too reliant on Locally Engaged Staff (LES) to do work that officers should be doing. For example, most consular sections assign LES to pre-screen applicants; e.g. examine documents, make sure the application is complete, etc. If a beleaguered or lazy FSO allows it, the pre-screening can slip quickly toward pre-approval of applicants. In one large North American post where this problem has been observed, many of the LES in the consular section are themselves immigrants from the same countries producing many of the "problem" applications at that post. In another post, this time a high-volume, high-fraud post in Asia, the American officers allowed the LES to complete the fingerprinting of applicants, in outright violation of regulations. The matter of LES is a very sensitive subject in the State Department, but nevertheless needs to be seriously examined. While many of the LES have years of experience and loyal service, and sometimes know the laws and regulations better than the American officers, it is also true that they have not undergone as thorough a background check, and may have ties to their community that run deeper than loyalty to their employer. The LES typically have been in their jobs a very long time, while the American staff turn over frequently, and this may add to both the temptation and the opportunity for them to become involved in criminal activity such as fraudulently obtaining visas.

With all the post 9/11 procedural changes and pressure to improve its performance, it would have been reasonable to expect the State Department to submit a budget request that reflects that priority, but that has not been the case. In its 2005 budget request, State has asked for funding for 63 new consular positions. Last year it asked for 68. That amounts to only about a 10 percent increase in consular officers, at a time when both the workload and public expectations for security and service are dramatically increasing. Indeed, State's own pre-9/11 workforce planning assessment, resulting in the Diplomatic Readiness Initiative, concluded that the Department needed to add nearly 400 positions to address its staffing crisis. At this rate, it will take at least another five years before State has enough personnel to do its job well. I can't recall another case of a government agency so unenthusiastic about hiring more staff.

The size of the consular corps is not the only human resource issue at State. Equally important is the fact that most consular officers are doing the work because they have to, not because they like it. The bulk of the routine adjudications work is handled by new junior officers on a mandatory consular assignment, who have had limited training and probably no experience in this kind of work. Most feel no particular calling to consular work, and are simply putting up with it on the way to an assignment in a different cone. While many are truly dedicated to their job and sincerely try to do the best they can, this arrangement is not a recipe for consistently high quality adjudications.

The State Department still clings to the idea that the visa function is best performed by generalist foreign service officers "who can put consular work in a broader context," as its personnel office puts it. I believe the nation would be far better served if visa adjudications instead were performed by a corps of visa specialists who chose this work as a career. There are two possible ways to accomplish this: either transform the consular cone into a specialty cone within State, like security, financial management, information technology, and personnel, or move the entire visa operation over to the Department of Homeland Security (DHS), so that the visa policy and processing responsibility will be all under one logical roof.

Policies. Having the best technology and staff to do immigration work is important, but it is not quite enough. The agencies charged with homeland security and Congress must also provide a policy framework that allows these two tools to be effective, and avoid adopting policies that undermine successful new security initiatives.

For instance, the new USVISIT system has greatly enhanced our capacity to identify known terrorists, criminals, and other immigration law violators. Yet the DHS has chosen to have it cover only a small proportion of those who enter the country. Most Canadians, Mexicans, and Visa Waiver Program (VWP) visitors are not now and not slated to be recorded in USVISIT. These groups represent more than half of the total admissions in 2003. This policy has been adopted despite our understanding that some terrorists, such as shoe-bomber Richard Reid, have tried to enter under VWP, that al-Quaeda supports terrorist cells in Canada, and that dodgy groups of Middle Easterners have attempted entry via Mexico. Many of these arrivals are checked against watch lists at the port of entry, but unless they are recorded by USVISIT, they cannot be flagged easily as overstayers. In addition, anyone claiming to be a U.S. citizen is exempt from USVISIT. Gaining entry as a U.S. citizen is easier than one might imagine. Under current operating procedures, it is possible to be admitted as a U.S. citizen on evidence as thin as an unverifiable personal affidavit.

Moreover, DHS has no intention of keeping USVISIT up and running if the lines at the airport should get too long. According to a DHS memorandum leaked to the news media, if the port of entry clearance process begins to slow down, immigration officers will gradually relax USVISIT standards to the point where only those in the highest threat categories will actually be fingerprinted and photographed.

DHS has backed off a number of other reforms proposed soon after 9/11. For example, In April 2002, the INS announced its intention to revise the rules on how long visitors will be permitted to stay. Until then, foreign tourists were routinely granted a six-month stay. The INS had concluded that this policy greatly contributed to the overstay problem and provided terrorists, drug dealers and other undesirable visitors with too long a period of time to carry on their illegal business before coming to the attention of immigration authorities. INS proposed awarding tourists a 30-day stay, unless the visitor could demonstrate a legitimate compelling reason to stay longer. Agency statistics showed that only about one-fourth of all tourists would be affected by the change. Following an intense lobbying campaign against the proposal by immigrant advocates and foreign vacation homeowners, however, the idea was quietly dropped in the transition into DHS.

In addition to displaying a certain timidity toward letting effective systems work as intended, both of the primary immigration agencies tolerate far too much fraud in the system. Part of this is a result of inadequate staffing, as previously discussed, but mostly it is a result of misplaced priorities. The State Department is only now in its 2005 budget proposing to establish a central unit devoted exclusively to nonimmigrant visa fraud, although this has been a problem probably for as long as NIVs have been issued. The low priority accorded to fraud is also reflected in the lack of meaningful consequences that fall on those who resort to fraud or misrepresentation in the application process. The regulations severely limit the kind of fraud that can be punished; for instance, lying about your identity, address, or previous applications is not considered important enough to be punished. Waivers that excuse previous immigration law transgressions are easily obtainable—"practically routine," for anyone with a relative here, according to a senior BCIS officer serving in a regional office. We cannot expect that this laxity toward fraud and deceit will be overlooked by terrorists any more than it is overlooked by the millions of others around the world who seek to enter the United States but cannot qualify under the law.

Finally, the biggest policy-related problem that threatens our ability to keep out terrorists is the fact that our immigration benefits programs are outrageously overbooked. For many years the United States has been offering immigration benefits to far more people than can be possibly accommodated within the limits of the law, which represents the number that we have decided we can absorb. For those with approved petitions, the wait for a green card or immigrant visa can be between three and 22 years. The BCIS is currently facing a backlog of more than five million applications, of which more than three million are for new immigrants, most of whom are already living here, many of whom have violated the law. Not only are these backlogs frustrating to legitimate applicants and their sponsors, they impede the effective screening of applicants, as officers are pressured to move cases through as quickly as possible. Even worse, by allowing people to remain here in limbo-like status, waiting years for approval and ignored if their application is turned down, the backlogs foster disrespect for the agency, its staff and the law itself.

The current administration sees there is a problem, and has asked Congress to approve spending an additional $160 million next year to address it. Unfortunately, the White House and some in Congress have also suggested adding a new so-called temporary guestworker program that could easily bring in another six to ten million applicants, either on top of or in front of the current backlog of cases.

The backlogs and waiting lists are not the result of agency incompetence or outmoded management techniques. They are the result of a series of deliberate policy choices: the IRCA amnesty, 245(i), and the LIFE Act. These programs brought millions of illegal aliens into the immigration queue, and undoubtedly contributed to the increases in new illegal immigration over the last decade. They also legalized terrorists, making it much easier for them to obtain their training overseas and go about the business of planning attacks on Americans. No staff increases, no web-based application process, no automated phone system, no imaginable amount of additional funding could possibly keep up with the crush of applicants that would arrive under the kind of new large-scale guestworker programs that have been proposed. Such a program would be as great a threat to our security as any of the other immigration policy weaknesses that have been discussed.

None of the problems I have touched on—technology, personnel, or policy—presents an insurmountable hurdle to the immigration agencies, all of which are blessed with smart and dedicated staff. What has been lacking is the will within the leadership to admit its mistakes and fundamentally change the way immigration work has been done.

Mr. GALLEGLY. Thank you, Ms. Vaughan.

Mr. Nunez, welcome.

STATEMENT OF THE HONORABLE PETER K. NUNEZ, DEPARTMENT OF POLITICAL SCIENCE AND INTERNATIONAL RELATIONS, UNIVERSITY OF SAN DIEGO

Mr. NUNEZ. Thank you, Mr. Chairman.

Mr. Chairman, distinguished Members of the Committee, you have my statement and I apologize for the version you have which has some typos in it but there is a corrected version which I hope makes it into the official record.

I would like to summarize my statement by focusing on three different components. First, we spent a lot of time talking about the failures of the visa program since 9/11. Clearly that is an area that deserves and requires significant additional work to solve or to fix.

My question coming from San Diego is suppose we succeed? Suppose we are able to do all the things that Ms. Vaughan has suggested and that we are able to have our own manpower we need and we can keep terrorists from coming into the U.S. with a visa. What are they going to do, stay home? No, I think they are going to join the other millions of people who are able to come to this country across relatively open borders at Mexico and Canada.

If an illiterate, unsophisticated, uneducated peasant from Latin America can circumvent our border authorities and live peacefully in the United States for years and years and years, certainly a dedicated, well-financed, educated terrorist would have no problem doing the same thing.

My second concern after fixing the visa program problems is we still have to deal with the landlords. 2,000 miles from Mexico, 4,000 miles from Canada, and an additional 1,000 miles at the Alaska/Canadian border, plus hundreds if not thousands of coastline or island possessions, Atlantic and Pacific coastline which are almost virtually wide open.

Second issue, interior enforcement. It is bad enough that we have failed so miserably on the border and at the ports of entry, but it is to me a worse failure that we have completely abandoned any kind of interior enforcement program for about the last 15 years.

There was a time, and I know many of you have talked to border patrol and I asked officials who have been in the system for awhile who can tell you how they used to enforce the law away from the border. It was routine. It was normal. It was accepted. It was legitimate.

We have been pressured by special interest groups to abandon that so we have essentially no employer sanction enforcement. The law doesn't permit it. Even if it did, there is no will to do it. We could use our labor laws to solve much of our immigration problem but no one cares about it.

State and local police in many communities have been intimated out of cooperating and coordinating their activities with the border patrol and INS. That is a tragedy. How many potential terrorists are going to get stopped for a traffic violation or a speeding ticket by a local police officer who knows the person is here illegally and just passes them on. Writes them a ticket and lets

them proceed down the road. That apparently happened to at least one or two of the people that were involved in the 9/11 circumstance.

So interior enforcement has got to be a high priority to deal with the 8 to 12 million illegal aliens and however many of them, whatever the percentage is, who may also be terrorists or drug traffickers, or committing other crimes.

The third area I would mention is the series of issues related to intelligence. You are all well aware and have remarked about the problems of connecting the dots that we had before 9/11 and the efforts underway now to try to do a better job on that. Clearly that is a huge priority. But intelligence issues I think we can break down into three components; collection of intelligence, analysis of intelligence, and dissemination.

The analysis and dissemination wasn't real good before 9/11. Those problems generally relate to the multitude of agencies that we had that play a role in all of this that have to somehow be brought together in a fusion center, if you will. Some way that all of these watch lists and all of these databases can be coordinated so that all of the border agencies and anti-terrorist groups participate.

But the bigger problem may be in collection of intelligence, especially within the United States. We have a very well developed sense of concern about privacy issues, the limits of Government, the way we want people to infiltrate and conduct investigations internally.

We are apparently happy to let the FBI infiltrate organized crime and drug trafficking groups but we have less tolerance for their ability or letting them do that with groups that may be fermenting terrorism. There are a number of collection issues, some of which were addressed in the Patriot Act, but some of which remain and have to be addressed still.

Congressman Rohrabacher mentioned the connection of terrorism to illegal immigration. There is absolutely no question about that. I would just add to that drug trafficking. The same borders that allow illegal immigrants and terrorists, drug traffickers to enter. Obviously it is the same problem. Is it fair to treat Mexico and Canada differently?

Well, I think as long—up until the point that Canada starts sending us tons and tons of drugs and hundreds and thousands of millions of illegal aliens, yes, I think it is fair to treat them differently. The threat is different on the two borders so clearly we have to treat the two borders differently. It is not an inherent character trait of Canadians or Mexicans. It is a problem of enforcement and the rule of law.

With Mexico the correction problems along the border are well documented. Thankfully, luckily we don't see that in Canada so clearly we have to treat the two borders differently until one of them improves or one of them gets as bad as the other. I hope it is not the latter. Thank you.

[The prepared statement of Mr. Nunez follows:]

PREPARED STATEMENT OF THE HONORABLE PETER K. NUNEZ, DEPARTMENT OF POLITICAL SCIENCE AND INTERNATIONAL RELATIONS, UNIVERSITY OF SAN DIEGO

Thank you for inviting me to testify today on this critical topic relating to the threat posed to the United States by international terrorism. The tragic events of September 11, 2001, are but the most dramatic example of the porousness of our borders and ports of entry, and the absolute folly of the border security "policies" that have marked our approach to border issues for most of the past 40 years, since the rewriting of our immigration laws in 1965.

My perspective on the issues being examined by this hearing are the product of my experience as a federal prosecutor in the Southern District of California beginning in 1972 and extending through my service as the United States Attorney during the Reagan Administration, ending in 1988; by my service as the Assistant Secretary of the Treasury for Enforcement during the first Bush Administration from 1990 to 1993; and my current employment as a lecturer in the Department of Political Science and International Relations at the University of San Diego, where I teach on "Transnational Crime and Terrorism" and the "Politics of Immigration Policy."

As a federal prosecutor in San Diego, I was regularly involved in the prosecution of violations of our immigration, customs, and drug laws, which brought me into close contact with our federal border agencies, including the Immigration and Naturalization Service, the Border Patrol, the Customs Service, the Drug Enforcement Administration, and the Federal Bureau of Investigation. Part of my responsibilities as the U.S. Attorney was to coordinate the overlapping activities of these and other agencies.

As the Assistant Secretary of the Treasury for Enforcement, I was responsible for all the law enforcement activities of the Treasury Department components, including the Customs Service, the Secret Service, the Bureau of Alcohol, Tobacco and Firearms, the Federal Law Enforcement Training Center, and the criminal investigations functions of the Internal Revenue Service. The Office of Foreign Assets Control, responsible for administering the various sanctions programs imposed on rogue nations by the United States, was also part of my office. During my tenure at Treasury, I oversaw the standup of the Financial Crimes Enforcement Network, a multi-agency anti-money laundering and financial crimes intelligence system. I also served as the Chairman of what was then called the Southwest Border Committee, which consisted of the Commissioners of Customs and INS and the Administrator of DEA, with the responsibility of coordinating all of the federal law enforcement activities along the southwest border with Mexico. I also presided over the initiation of Project NorthStar, a multi-agency coordinating mechanism on the U.S./Canadian border including the border law enforcement agencies in the United States and Canada. All of these duties have given me the opportunity to observe the difficulties we face as a nation in trying to enforce our laws along our borders to protect the American public from the horrors of illegal drugs, terrorists, and rampant illegal immigration.

This nation began to lose control of its borders following the passage of the 1965 amendments to the 1952 Immigration and Nationality Act, which had the perverse affect of stimulating both legal and illegal immigration simultaneously. The end of the Bracero Program occurred at approximately the same time, as did the onset of the counter culture and the explosion of the use of illegal drugs, most of which were produced outside the United States and smuggled across our borders. None of the agencies responsible for the enforcement of our immigration or drug laws were prepared for the deluge of illegal acts that soon overwhelmed them, and Congress was slow to respond with the necessary manpower, equipment and other resources necessary to combat these evils. The result was that our borders were overrun, illegal drugs were easily available, and illegal immigration became a routine part of the American experience.

By the 1980's, it was clear that both our drug policies and our immigration policies had failed miserably, and efforts were undertaken by successive administrations and Congresses to turn the tide. Improvements were made in our drug laws and the agencies responsible for combating this problem, but it was a case of too little too late. As for the flaws in our immigration policy, Congressional action designed to end this debacle failed completely; the 1986 Immigration Reform and Control Act, with its three-pronged approach of (1) employer sanctions, (2) enhanced border enforcement, and (3) an amnesty for millions of illegal aliens, not only failed to cure the problems it was designed to address, it indirectly led to even more immigration—both legal and illegal.

Employer sanctions failed completely as a deterrent to illegal immigration, due to the inherent weaknesses in the law as written, and also due to the considerable pressure applied to INS by pro-immigrant and pro-business special interests through political channels. Subsequent efforts in Congress to remedy the deficiencies in this law were defeated by those profiting from the immigration chaos that had resulted. Border security continued to be ignored into the 1990's, when Congress finally began to increase the size of the Border Patrol, doubling it from around 4,000 agents in 1993 to more than 9,000 by the late '90's. And approximately 2.7 million illegal aliens were given amnesty in the 5 years following passage of IRCA in 1986.

But during this same time Congress added to the problem by enacting amendments to the immigration laws in 1990 which have resulted in unprecedented increases in the number of immigrants allowed entry to the United States. We are currently experiencing the highest sustained period of immigration in our nation's history, further straining the resources of the INS. Interior enforcement—the term used to describe what used to be the routine enforcement of our immigration laws away from the borders—was almost completely abandoned by INS during the last 15 years, under intense pressure from the same political interest groups mentioned above. And state and local politicians have exacerbated the problem by instructing their police officials to either ignore immigration violations they discover, or refuse to cooperate with INS officials, or both, as they continue to cater to special interests at the local level.

The INS—never a model of efficiency or effectiveness—was now completely overwhelmed, and undermined by special interests intent on making sure that INS would never be able to perform its congressionally-mandated functions. Business interests dependent on an unending flow of cheap, exploitable, labor; immigrant groups intent on keeping the door open so that more of their relatives, friends, and countrymen would be allowed to enter; immigration lawyers who derive personal profit from the plight of immigrants; the politicians who rely on these interests groups for their continued reelection; all of these groups joined together to deprive INS of the resources and legal authority needed to implement the immigration laws in a coherent fashion.

As the United States struggled to deal with the problems of cross-border drug trafficking, illegal immigration, and the processing of record numbers of legal immigrants, along came yet another problem of epic proportions—international terrorism. The success of these groups in infiltrating the United States first became clear in 1993 with the first bombing of the World Trade Center, but became a sign of the complete disintegration of our border security apparatus after the tragic events of

9/11. Finally an event of unspeakable horror caught the attention of our elected leaders and has led us to begin the process of rebuilding a border security system designed to protect us from future catastrophe.

Certainly the creation of the Department of Homeland Security was a step in the right direction. Combining all of the agencies involved in border security issues—Customs, INS, and the Border Patrol—in one department should lead to enhanced enforcement at the border, and better coordination between agencies with similar but different missions and priorities. The omission from DHS of the FBI, or at least that part of the FBI that is the primary anti-terrorism component of our entire federal government structure, is odd, to say the least, given the overarching mission of DHS to protect us from terrorism, but that oddity does not detract from the positive aspects achieved by combining the border interdiction agencies.

And one note of caution regarding the possible advantages of combining these agencies into one department: the fact that these agencies are now all part of the same department does not automatically solve all of the problems experienced in the past when they were part of different Cabinet-level departments. After all, both the FBI and the INS were part of the same Justice Department on 9/11, yet the post 9/11 analysis demonstrated serious gaps in the sharing of information between these two Justice Department agencies. Moving boxes around on an organizational chart does not—by itself—create an environment of cooperation and information sharing. How DHS fulfills the espectations that it will share information internally between and among its constituent parts is yet to be demonstrated.

Further, with regard to the sharing of intelligence, this has proven to be a huge problem for law enforcement agencies in the past, and an even bigger problem when the sharing of information must include non-law enforcement agencies such as the Central Intelligence Agency, the National Security Agency, the Department of Defense, and the State Department, all of whom play some role in protecting us from future terrorist attacks. These are not frivolous issues, and the problems in sharing intelligence go well beyond the parochial nature of federal agencies. How this process is managed in the future will have much to do with how successful we are in preventing another 9/11.

It is my belief that you cannot approach the issue of protecting America from future terrorist attacks as an isolated issue, that it is necessary to consider the broader issue of border security to include terrorism, immigration enforcement, and drug trafficking as a whole. Because the same deficiencies that exist—at least along our borders and ports of entry—that would allow a terrorist to gain entry to the U.S. are the same deficiencies that allow for the entry of millions of illegal aliens and many thousands of pounds of illegal drugs every year. After all, if hundreds of thousands of illiterate, unskilled, uneducated peasants from the interior of various Latin American countries can successfully navigate the holes in our borders and ports of entry to successfully take up residence inside the United States and remain here indefinitely, what makes anyone believe that a more sophisticated, better financed, and dedicated member of a terrorist cell could not do the same thing? If international drug traffickers can successfully smuggle hundreds of thousands of pounds of cocaine, marijuana, heroin, amphetamines, and other illegal drugs into the U.S., why is it not equally likely that a terrorist group could successfully smuggle a few pounds or gallons of biological, chemical, or nuclear material into this country? How many illegal aliens stopped by local police for a traffic violation and released under a local policy which provides sanctuary for illegal aliens could be tomorrow's terrorist? Which student admitted on a temporary visa who overstays that visa, or in fact never shows up for school, will be the next terrorist to kill Americans?

It is my understanding that approximately 500 million people enter the United States each year (or more specifically, there are 500 million "entries"), and approximately 8 million containers are brought into the U.S. through our various seaports annually. This is indeed a formidible challenge to our Homeland Security authorities, but its size cannot and should not be the sole determining factor in how we protect ourselves from the threat of terrorism. We as a Nation must do what we have to do to protect ourselves—that must be our first priority. If there is a way to protect ourselves that minimizes the impact on the speed with which people and containers are admitted, that would be our preferred option. But we must finally abandon the notion that it is more important to allow people and containers to enter the U.S. quickly and easily than it is to protect ourselves from future terrorist attacks, increased availability of harmful drugs, and the demonstrably harmful effects of illegal immigration.

This country must remember that is is based upon the concept of the rule of law. We are a nation of laws—we must abide by the laws we have adopted to deal with the problems of immigration, drugs, and terrorism. It is not enough to pass laws in Congress or in the state legislatures and then ignore them because we are afraid of offending special interests or because of notions of political correctness. And there is no way a country can fight a war against terrorism when it ignores its borders, refuses to enforce its laws away from the borders, and provides sanctuary or informal immunity to those who have broken our laws by coming here illegally or staying beyond there welcome.

Since 9/11 we have paid a great deal of attention to the visa issuing process‘ and to the creation of a system designed to keep better track of those we admit as non-immigrants. This is all well and good. But let us suppose that we are completely successful in that regard, and that we can implement a full-proof system for admitting only those that mean us no harm, and that we succeed in keeping track of those we admit to make sure they depart as scheduled. Of all of the many problems that need to be addressed, that is the easiest part, because all of those applicants for admission go through a controlled environment, from an overseas embassy or consuate, to a port of entry at an airport or seaport, where the physical process of inspection can be completely controlled. Technology is of its greatest assistance in this setting, and if we wish, can provide a very high degree of reliability and security.

So what alternative means of entry do terrorists look to if we close the door on them at the ports of entry and the visa process? As long as our land borders with Mexico and Canada remain as open as they now are, terrorists can enter the U.S. as easily as any of the hundreds of thousands of illegal aliens who regularly shred our land border security.

Canadian security officials have long-admitted that there are approximately 50 terrorist groups operating in Canada. The border between Canada and the “Lower 48” states is 4,000 miles long, and was patrolled by 300 Border Patrol agents on 9/11 (now increased to 1,000 agents). Throw in the additional 1,000 mile border between Canada and Alaska and you have a huge hole in the dike.

Corruption in Mexico and along the U.S./Mexican border is so pervasive that international drug cartels operate with near-impunity in that environment. Are we so naive as to suspect that the right amount of money could not purchace the entry of a few terrorists from time to time?

And consider the thousands of miles of coastline that are virtually wide open; thousands of miles of Atlantic Coast; thousands of miles of Pacific Coast; thousands of miles of coastline around Hawaii and our island possessions. Once a terrorist enters any of these islands surreptiously in the dark of night, he can then travel via airline to the mainland U.S. without passing through any immigration or Customs checks.

In short, efforts to strengthen our visa and passport control process should be a high priority, but we must recognize that our open borders will continue to make us vulnerable until we stiffen them to the maximum degree possible. And beyond a better border security apparatus we need to allow Homeland Security officials to restart their interior enforcement functions, free of political interference, and with the aid—compelled if necessary—of local law enforcement personnel. Anything that allows illegal aliens to avoid the consequences of their illegal acts should be eliminated; by reducing the ease with which those who have broken our laws can remain in place will enable us to provide a more secure homeland for all.

Mr. GALLEGLY. Thank you very much, Mr. Nunez.

STATEMENT OF BILL WEST, CONSULTANT, THE INVESTIGATIVE PROJECT

Mr. WEST. Thank you, Mr. Chairman. I would like to thank the Committee and the staff for the opportunity to give testimony today. I have submitted my formal statement and given the time constraints, again, I would like to summarize my statement to cover several topics here in the time period.

Border security really is more of an illusion than it is a reality. I think the clearest evidence of that, as Mr. Nunez just mentioned, is the fact that every day thousands of unskilled, un sophisticated farm laborers manage to penetrate our border defenses. It would be foolish to believe that sophisticated terrorists with access to support networks, illicit funds, smuggling organizations, and a myriad of false identity documents cannot also penetrate those same border defenses.

They do, they have, and they are here already. That has been demonstrated many times over. Given that, I believe we have a state of affairs with border security that clearly indicates that we have limited border security circumstances here in the United States.

Border intercepts of terrorist suspects is a fairly rare event. That does not reflect negatively on our border enforcers so much as it is an indicator of the sheer volume of human traffic that comes through legitimate ports of entry.

Literally hundreds of millions of persons crossing ports of entry every year and a certain set of circumstances with policies and procedures, at least pre-9/11 and, to a large extent, currently that moves more toward moving commerce, both human and cargo, than it does to affect proper border security efforts.

The interception, if you will, of the millennium bomber, Ahmed Ressam and the interception in Orlando in August 2001 of Mohammed al Kahtami, the suspected 20th hijacker by an alert INS inspector are two examples where border enforcers and inspectors have succeeded obviously in capturing suspected terrorists. That is obviously a good thing.

But, notwithstanding these events, these fairly isolated incidents usually terrorist suspects are captured as the result of interior counterterrorism investigations that are conducted once these suspects have already made it past the border. Another clear indication that border security lacks in the ability to actually capture foreign terrorists.

Much has been said about the USVISIT program. the USVISIT program, I believe, is a very good first step. It is a long overdue first step. However, the USVISIT program, as the Government has officially stated, is really a controlled process for controlling the entry and departure of nonimmigrant aliens into and out of the United States.

Until the departure control process or function of USVISIT is fully implemented, the USVISIT will only be partially successful. Even assuming the technology works, and hopefully it will, once the departure control element of USVISIT is fully implemented, if it is, that allows for the issue of a whole other set of—that allows for a whole other set of issues to arise.

As Congressman Tancredo has alluded to, nearly half the illegal alien population in the United States entered the United States legitimately on temporary visas. Presumably USVISIT at some point once departure control is implemented would identify a very large number of overstayed violators. Who will actually enforce those violators? Who is going to pursue those violators? These are issues that I don't believe have yet been addressed and should be addressed.

Another issue is the inheritance, if you will, by DHS of a system of databases from INS, computer databases that were inherently inaccurate, did not speak to each other, did not interface with each other. Dozens of database systems that were never fixed in spite of hundreds of millions of dollars devoted to that problem by Congress. Years of effort by the agency to try to fix the problem that never was fixed. That remains a problem.

And, finally, I would like to address, or bring to your attention the validizing, if you will, of immigration law enforcement. That has been an issue for decades that was always a problem that never allowed for the nationalization, if you will, of proper immigration enforcement efforts. It continues to this day. The Department of Homeland Security now is responsible for immigration law enforcement efforts. The Interior Enforcement Branch, the Immigration and Customs Enforcement Agency is a multifaceted agency that is still trying to evolve into mission accomplishment and that is an issue that needs to still be in trust.

I see my time is up so I will move on. Thank you.

[The prepared statement of Mr. West follows:]

PREPARED STATEMENT OF BILL WEST, CONSULTANT, THE INVESTIGATIVE PROJECT

I would like to thank the Chairman, the Committee members and the staff for the privilege and opportunity to provide testimony at this hearing today.

Border security and especially preventing the entry of foreign terrorists into the United States are clearly issues critical to our national security. Unfortunately, our border security is more illusion than reality. America's border defenses are penetrated thousands of times a day by unsophisticated, unskilled and uneducated foreign laborers. It would be foolish to assume foreign terrorists, with access to sophisticated support networks, substantial illicit funds, smuggling organizations and routes and a myriad of false identity documents would find it difficult to enter the United States. In fact, such terrorists find our borders to be barely an inconvenience.

Border intercepts of terrorists are rare exceptions and not the rule. Cases identifying such suspects generally result from multi-agency counter-terrorism investigative efforts conducted within the interior of the U.S. well after these suspects have entered. The case of Mahmoud Youssef Kourani, an alleged Lebanese Hezbollah operative indicted in Detroit last year for terrorism support charges, who was found to have been smuggled across the U.S. Mexican border, is a recent example.

Occasionally, however, the efforts of our border enforcement personnel pay off. The capture of Millennium Bomber Ahmed Ressam on the Northwest border with Canada and the interception of suspected 9/11 20th hijacker Mohamed al-Qahtani by an INS Inspector in Orlando in August 2001 are two such examples. Again, these are rare events. The sheer volume of human inspectional traffic, on the order of hundreds of millions per year through legitimate ports of entry, belies any ability to conduct a thorough security screening. The average immigration inspection, before the implementation of the US VISIT program, took about forty seconds, and officials have boasted that US VISIT has only added fifteen seconds to the process. That itself is telling about where the priorities really are. Pre-9/11, the Federal inspectional system was focused more on moving commerce, human and cargo, than on securing the borders. Among the management ranks of INS Inspectors in the field, the general attitude was, "Crank 'em in." While there have been efforts to change that mindset since 9/11, moving the inspectional line at a quick pace is still a high priority.

US VISIT is a long overdue step in the right direction. Combining biometrics with border security efforts is a must. Assuming the technology actually works, and given the history of U.S. Immigration authorities and technological innovation—that is a concern; but if it works, the system could eventually prove to be a powerful national security tool. The system has already identified and captured several fugitive criminals; however, it was primarily designed to control nonimmigrant alien entrants. For that to happen, the departure control portion of the system must be made to fully work. Once departure control is fully implemented, another universe of issues arises. It is generally recognized that close to half of the illegal alien population in the U.S. entered through ports of entry on temporary visas and simply overstayed their time. Given that, eventually US VISIT would presumably identify very large numbers of non-departure violators. What will happen with that information? Will there be any intelligence triage? Will there be any enforcement action against those violators; and if so, by whom? Will the violator leads be placed in any law enforcement lookout systems? Or, will nothing be done and US VISIT simply becomes another border security White Elephant?

Another issue plaguing border and immigration enforcers is the issue of databases. The inefficiencies and inaccuracies of the computer systems of the former INS were notorious well before the 9/11 tragedies. Recent 9/11 Commission hearings have brought to light how, far from originally reported, the 9/11 terrorists did not enter the U.S. on "clean" and "legal" visas, but several had in fact lied on their visa applications, making readily identifiable false statements. Others committed immigration law violations that should have been noticed and acted upon but were not. Much of this goes to the inability of the immigration and visa record systems to interface with each other. Within INS, its own databases were stand-alone systems that were not interconnected, that in spite of many years and hundreds of millions of dollars allocated by Congress to upgrade INS computer systems. Unfortunately, the Department of Homeland Security and its immigration-related agencies have inherited this legacy. This must be quickly fixed, and biometrics must be fully added to the visa and immigration benefit application process, as had been clearly recommended in Congressional testimony in 1997.

Finally, since 9/11, it is absolutely clear that immigration matters are directly linked to issues relative to international terrorism. Incredibly, before 9/11, the most senior INS officials failed to recognize that fact, and very few immigration enforcement resources were devoted to national security cases. The issue of politicizing immigration law enforcement continues even while we are in a war on terror. Combined with the institutional and structural problems within the immigration systems, some of which still exist, we are hamstringing the very national security processes meant to protect us. One clear example of caving into political correctness at the expense of security is the virtual abandonment of the utilization of classified evidence in Title-II immigration removal proceedings, as authorized under 8 C.F.R. 240.49, and bringing no cases under Title-V Alien Terrorist Removal Court proceedings. These proceedings, lawfully passed by Congress and on the books, are being ignored because special interest groups and certain media have mischaracterized what they are and how they could be employed, yet they could be powerful and narrowly focused enforcement tools brought to bear against foreign terror suspects.

In a time when America faces uncounted shadow enemies who are willing to die to kill us, and who have the means to slip past our borders with ease, those responsible for securing the borders and finding those threats who make it in, must have every legal weapon available to defend us, but those weapons also need to work properly.

Mr. GALLEGLY. Thank you, Mr. West.

STATEMENT OF PEGGY STERLING, VICE PRESIDENT, SAFETY, SECURITY AND ENVIRONMENTAL, AMERICAN AIRLINES

Ms. STERLING. Good morning, Mr. Chairman and the panel. I thank the Committee for this opportunity to represent American Airlines here today. I will give you a brief introductory statement and then be available to answer any of your questions.

While the horror and shock of September 11th have abated somewhat during the past 2½ years, the sadness endures. Twenty-three members of the American Airlines team died that day. Our hearts continue to go out to their families, and to the families of the passengers, firefighters, police officers, rescue workers, and military personnel who made the ultimate sacrifice to keep our country safe.

The courage summoned by so many people that day has both inspired us and strengthened our resolve to do whatever it takes to ensure that nothing like 9/11 ever happens again. Our industry is vital to interstate and international commerce. Our mission is to provide safe and secure transportation for passengers, their baggage and cargo.

American and its affiliates serve more than 250 cities in more than 40 countries around the world. We appreciate the work that Congress is doing and the leadership it is providing to strengthen the security of our aviation system. At American Airlines, the safety and security of our passengers and employees is first and foremost in any decision we make.

While safety comes first, our commitment to security is a fundamental part of our daily operations. From our passenger service representatives, to our in-flight crews to our station managers and to our ground security personnel; American's dedicated professionals are committed to maintaining the highest level of safety and security, as well as providing excellent customer service.

In the interest of time, I will not focus on the roles of the Government or the airline industry as it relates to the aviation security system in the pre-9/11 environment. Suffice it to say that at that time the Federal Aviation Administration set the security standards for U.S. airports, U.S. airlines, and foreign carriers flying into the United States.

American has always taken very seriously the importance of its role in implementing the system that the FAA designed and enforced. Today, we continue to rely on the FAA, the Transportation Security Administration and other U.S. Government agencies responsible for counter-terrorism, intelligence, and law enforcement. We rely on their threat assessments for the formulation of industry security strategy and for the design of countermeasures to address those threats.

The civil aviation industry did not foresee the type of attacks that took place on September 11th. It is clear that neither domestic nor international security measures were designed to deal with coordinated, suicidal hijack teams. However, much progress has been made since September 11th, and I commend the FAA, the Department of Homeland Security, the TSA, and other Government agencies for all their ongoing efforts to strengthening our national security.

As we continue to pursue our mission of providing safe, secure air travel for our passengers in the midst of a global war on terrorism, the events of September 11th remind us to be vigilant and to constantly evaluate, and continuously improve our aviation security system.

All of us at American Airlines applaud the work of Congress and appreciate the work of this Committee to further strengthen our border security. What we learn from hearings such as this, and how we apply the lessons from 9/11, will make air travel and our country safer and more secure.

We all must ensure that our aviation system is closed to those individuals who would harm us but open to those who are dedicated to global commerce.

Thank you for the opportunity to appear before the Committee today and I will be happy to answer your questions.

[The prepared statement of Ms. Sterling follows:]

PREPARED STATEMENT OF PEGGY STERLING, VICE PRESIDENT, SAFETY, SECURITY AND ENVIRONMENTAL, AMERICAN AIRLINES

Good Morning, Mr. Chairman and Members of the Subcommittee. My name is Peggy Sterling, and I am Vice President—Safety, Security and Environmental for American Airlines. I am responsible for American's Security Department and I report directly to Bob Reding, American's Senior Vice President—Technical Operations. I thank the Committee for this opportunity to represent American Airlines here today. I will give a brief introductory statement and then be available to answer your questions.

While the horror and shock of September 11th have abated somewhat during the past two and a half years, the sadness endures. Twenty-three members of the American Airlines team died that day. Our hearts continue to go out to their families, and to the families of the passengers, firefighters, police officers, rescue workers, and military personnel who made the ultimate sacrifice to keep our country safe.

The courage summoned by so many people that day has both inspired us and strengthened our resolve to do whatever it takes to ensure that nothing like 9/11 ever happens again. Our industry is vital to interstate and international commerce. Our mission is to provide safe and secure transportation for passengers, their baggage and cargo. American and its affiliates serve more than 250 cities in more than 40 countries around the world.

We appreciate the work that Congress is doing—and the leadership it is providing—to strengthen the security of our aviation system. At American Airlines, the safety and security of our passengers and employees is first and foremost in any decision we make. While safety comes first, our commitment to security is a fundamental part of our daily operations. From our passenger service representatives, to our in-flight crews to our station managers and to our ground security personnel; American's dedicated professionals are committed to maintaining the highest level of safety and security, as well as providing excellent customer service.

In the interest of time, I will not focus on the roles of the government or the airline industry as it relates to the aviation security system in the pre-9/11 environment. Suffice it to say that at that time the Federal Aviation Administration set the security standards for U.S. airports, U.S. airlines, and foreign carriers flying into the United States.

American has always taken very seriously the importance of its role in implementing the system that the FAA designed and enforced. Today, we continue to rely on the FAA, the Transportation Security Administration and other U.S. government agencies responsible for counter-terrorism, intelligence, and law enforcement. We rely on their threat assessments for the formulation of industry security strategy and for the design of countermeasures to address those threats.

The civil aviation industry did not foresee the type of attacks that took place on September 11th. It is clear that neither domestic nor international security measures were designed to deal with coordinated, suicidal hijack teams. However, much progress has been made since September 11th, and I commend the FAA, the Department of Homeland Security, the TSA, and other government agencies for all their ongoing efforts to strengthening our nation's security.

As we continue to pursue our mission of providing safe, secure air travel for our passengers—in the midst of a global war on terrorism—the events of September 11th remind us to be vigilant and to constantly evaluate, and continuously improve our aviation security system.

All of us at American Airlines applaud the work of Congress and appreciate the work of this Committee to further strengthen our border security. What we learn from hearings such as this, and how we apply the lessons from 9/11, will make air travel—and our country—safer and more secure.

We all must ensure that our aviation system is closed to those individuals who would harm us but open to those who are dedicated to global commerce.

Thank you for the opportunity to appear before the committee today and I will be happy to answer your questions.

Mr. GALLEGLY. Thank you, Ms. Sterling.

First of all, Mr. West, I would like to respond to something that you mentioned about the issue of interdiction on a positive note. While it is a rare situation that we catch folks at the border, in my opening statement you may have heard that I acknowledge the fact that through a very capable border patrol agent up at the Canada/Washington State border we interdicted an individual that had plans and the ability to take out this very airport at the millennium so there are some positive stories. While we are focusing on trying to get to resolution of other things, it is also important to play up some of the positive things that folks are doing.

Mr. WEST. Absolutely.

Mr. GALLEGLY. Mr. Nunez, thank you for your service. I followed your career for many years and I have great respect for the job that you have done. As we discussed earlier, 13 of the 19 9/11 hijackers were found to have had doctored or fraudulent passports or other documents with suspicious indicators. As you may know, in the bill we produced in 1996 we made the penalties for counterfeiting documents or for using documents the same as for counterfeiting or using currency.

As a former United States Attorney would you say that the United States Government is doing an adequate job in prosecuting the manufacturing or use of counterfeit documents the same as they would counterfeit currency?

Mr. NUNEZ. Mr. West may be able to add to this but I am sure that the prosecutors are willing to accept and prosecute cases that are brought to their attention. I know that INS and the FBI and, to some lesser degree, DHS now also, look upon the commercial or the large manufacturers of documents as a priority.

I mean, I have seen plenty of cases prosecuted along those lines. But the individual cases, I think, would really be prosecuted. In other words, if someone was caught with a document, the U.S. Attorneys most of the time would say it is not worth the time to bring the case to court.

Now, there are ways to handle that. In San Diego where we handle large volumes of cases in the past, if you charge somebody with an offense that has a high penalty called for by the law but there is a lower plea bargaining circumstance available, you can process a lot of cases if you let the people plead to a lesser charge. You can theoretically handle a fairly large number but I don't think that is the priority of any of the agencies is to deal with individual cases of document fraud. You are usually looking at the manufacturers, the distributors, the sellers.

Mr. GALLEGLY. But would you not agree that if we started prosecuting some of these folks that are buying their documents down on Alvarado Street—and I can give you the market places in my home district. You know where they are on every corner working out of vans, mobile offices—if we started prosecuting the users, kind of like they do johns with prostitution cases, would it be an effective way to deal with the issue?

Mr. NUNEZ. Yes, and it would not be—it would take resources but not an overly—you could do it very creatively.

Mr. GALLEGLY. Ms. West, I want to thank you again very much for being the only representive from the airline industry here today. I have a question for you. I know you have been in operations and familiar with the operation of American for a long, long time. I have a lot of miles with American as I do with United and others as a flyer who goes back and forth every week and ½ for 18 years, as my colleagues up here will attest and they do as well.

I ran into a situation back prior to 9/11 where we had flight attendants and pilots from American Airlines contacting my office about a policy that they said that American had in place, and maybe other airlines as well, from an operational standpoint that it is common, I guess, that you have excess tickets sometimes on flights that go unsold.

Are you familiar with a process whereby a block of tickets would be sold when there was, let us say, on the red eye at 10 o'clock at night from LA to Washington, DC where there were 50 empty seats on the airplane and ½ hour before the flight or whatever they would sell those as a block. Have you ever heard of anything like that?

Ms. STERLING. No, sir.

Mr. GALLEGLY. That is interesting because I had flight attendants coming to us giving us information that on the red eye flight from LA to Washington/Dulles it was a common practice to sell a block of tickets for a very low price to an agency. I won't say what business the individual was in. Let us just say a travel agent or coyote or something like that, and they would have people that get on the airplane every week with one little bag, many of which did not have any idea where they were going, spoke no English, and would get off the airplane in Washington, DC.

You might be interested to know that I had a meeting in my office, this is prior to 9/11, with Janet Reno and then commissioner of INS Doris Meizner, and I asked about this policy. I said I have flight attendants and pilots from American Airlines coming in and telling me this. I have seen first hand questionable activities as I would get on the red eye.

I asked Doris Meizner and Janet Reno that very question. The response I got from Janet Reno is, "Congressman, we are aware of this going on but we don't have the resources to deal with it." You as an operational person are not aware of American ever selling a block of tickets on any flights?

Ms. STERLING. What I can say is that we designate a certain number of seats for discounted seats and we inventory those. We don't do it generally the day of departure. Generally it is done in advance of departure.

Mr. GALLEGLY. Well, whatever. In any event, my understanding is that there were blocks, large blocks. Not just an individual who calls and says, "Can I get one of the discount seats?" Maybe a block of 20 or 25 or 35 seats.

Ms. STERLING. I really can't speak to how our revenue management system is set up, but I can tell you that we identify a certain number of seats to certain destinations.

Mr. GALLEGLY. My time is short. For the record, would you be kind enough to do a little research and see if historically—I am going to be asking other airlines the same question—historically American has ever had this policy of selling a block of discount tickets and if that procedure has changed post-9/11.

Ms. STERLING. We will check into it and get back to you.

Mr. GALLEGLY. Mr. Sherman.

Mr. SHERMAN. Ms. Vaughan, I am intrigued by your idea that we have a separate corps of people who are consular officials dealing with visas. I have had a lot of excellent extremely bright, well educated people work for me. They all want to joint the foreign service. They are going to be Ambassadors or they are going to work for world peace. They finally join the foreign service and, of course, they do a few years of visa work.

On the one hand, these folks don't have visas as their career objective. On the other hand, they are very bright capable folks. Would we be better off with people who wanted to be in visa operations their entire career, or would we be better off with a few years service from these very bright folks that want to move on to foreign affairs?

Ms. VAUGHAN. I think that we would be better off with consular work as an area of specialty. This is really not a new idea. I think back in the 1970s the State Department did augment its consular corps with people who are specialists and who wanted to be doing this work.

I agree with you. I think most people really do try and are conscientious. They try to do the best they can. Unfortunately, there are just as many perhaps, I don't know exactly because I haven't seen any polls taken but who really are just doing time because they don't have a long-term interest in consular work. They have a long-term interest in political or economic work or some other variety of consular experience.

Mr. SHERMAN. It comes down to the smartest person you can get or do you want the person who is most interested in the work they are doing. It may be a combination of those two with some very experienced people to devote their lives to consular work would make some sense.

I want to move on to Mr. West. We have got this whole effort to stop terrorist from coming into the United States. We deny 133 visas for the whole year. Even those folks may just be innocent folks deprived of an opportunity to visit Disneyland. I am not aware of any of them actually being arrested as terrorists by their host country so they are not like the 133 worst people in the world. They are just the 133 we didn't let in.

Is the visa process even relevant to keeping America safe from terrorists? I listened carefully to your testimony where you describe how people who come to the United States illegally, some of those on those blocks of flights that the Chairman was talking about, don't have a lot of money, don't go through a lot of training as to how to blend into the United States and don't bother to buy their tickets individually.

One wonders whether a sophisticated terrorist with money, and the 9/11 hijackers weren't all that sophisticated but even rudimentary sophistication plus cash isn't enough to—I mean, yes, as you point out, they are sophisticated enough to deal with what is a very haphazard enforcement system. Should we be devoting efforts to this whole visa evaluation process? Has it done us any good?

Mr. WEST. I think better efforts should be devoted to it. I think sometimes, occasionally the visa screening process works and prevents people from coming here. There are probably success stories where visas are denied that we don't hear about. I know that does happen. When I was on the job I saw that happen rarely, but it did happen.

Mr. SHERMAN. Well, if we just randomly deny 10 percent of all visa applications, actually we deny well over half of all visa applications as I understand it, from many countries, then we would be denying 10 percent or 15 percent of the terrorists.

Mr. WEST. Give a monkey enough baseballs.

Mr. SHERMAN. Now, the databases that we're working on for terrorist watch, is it your understanding that they reflect the law enforcement information of our foreign allies? It is not enough that the United States law enforcement thinks a particular person shouldn't be allowed in the United States. Do we have the Saudi Arabian list of people in their country that they are not real certain about.

Some of the intelligence databases includes some friendly allied database information but that does not include—I would not think would include like Saudi information to my knowledge. Our own internal database information, like I said, is very fractured and inaccurate when it comes to immigration record information. When it comes to intelligence database information, that is still a work in progress.

Mr. SHERMAN. There is this program of exit tracking. I am worried about not only the false negatives. That is to say, when people leave the country and we don't know they left. The kiosk at BWI, you could have a lot of false positives.

In other words, somebody could swipe three or four cards going through the kiosk and three of their friends could be identified, you know, records as being out of the United States when, in fact, they are still here. Do you think that just having people swipe a card without first reviewing the process is going to give us both the false positives and the false negatives?

Mr. WEST. A voluntary system is going to be an open invitation to fraud.

Mr. SHERMAN. Both in terms of people not swiping and people swiping several times. If we had a good system, would that provide a lot of good data for Homeland Security?

Mr. WEST. It would but then you have to determine what you do with the information.

Mr. SHERMAN. What should we do with the information?

Mr. WEST. If you had enough enforcement resources, you could follow up leads and enforce the law and pursue violators.

Mr. SHERMAN. Finally, what about our ability to infiltrate organizations with ties here in the United States or with personnel here in the United States where there is general support for terrorist actions against America? Some of those, I mean, your organization started with the Jihad of America documentary where you see hundreds of people gathered together to chant for the destruction of America. How effective are we in infiltrating those organizations? How can we be more effective?

Mr. WEST. Are you talking about the Government?

Mr. SHERMAN. Yes. We, the Government.

Mr. WEST. Well, again, it is a resource issue. From a legal standpoint post-9/11 it has gotten better with the Patriot Act. However, with the resource issue you've got, the agencies must have the manpower and the flexibility to devote those resources to those types of cases. Right now other than the FBI the Department of Homeland Security is limited with that.

Mr. SHERMAN. Finally, if we have limited resources, would you put them in the visa granting process or the infiltration process?

Mr. WEST. The infiltration/enforcement.

Mr. GALLEGLY. Mr. Rohrabacher.

Mr. ROHRABACHER. Thank you very much, Mr. Chairman. I am sorry that I will have to leave very quickly after my question time. I've got another meeting in Orange County but I appreciate what we have heard so far. Just a few observations. One is that I don't think that it is an excuse the fact that even if we make the immigration system 100 percent effective that it is not going to deal 100 percent with the terrorist threat. I don't consider that to be any excuse for not trying to deal with the immigration system.

In dealing with the immigration system it is out of control and broken and totally nonfunctioning right now there are terrorists who come in and we know that. At least, in fixing that we will at least limit one avenue that the terrorists have, terrorists who have targeted America have to come here and hurt us.

Let me say that credit cards that we have in our pocket are run by private organizations and they are able to have security systems that protect their assets operating instantaneously all over the world. I mean, if somebody uses a credit card some place like Tajikistan, within a few minutes the credit card in New York City knows something is wrong and people are acting on it.

There is something seriously wrong when the private sector can be that efficient and we can't even devise a system that is going to work with lots of people working together and a long time period. We don't even know if someone who has come into this country on a visa has left the country.

I checked on the number of people coming here from China, from mainland China, because I just had the sneaking suspicion that there were a lot of illegal immigrants from mainland China coming here. I don't know why I should think that. When you see Chinatowns springing up all over the United States, I don't why I would ever think that. Guess what? The number of visas issued dramatically increased over the last 10 years but we have no idea if any of them ever went back to China. We have no idea.

That is insane and there is bound to be in a situation like this with a flood of illegals coming into our country, there are bound to be people in that flood who, yes, most of them, the vast majority of them, about 99 percent of them probably are just like the other immigrants who came to this country. They are looking for wealth to improve their own opportunities and to improve the lives of their family.

If it is just 1 percent, we are in big trouble. If just 1 percent of the illegal immigrants are actually here to do something that might be what we now today would call terrorism, this country is in big trouble. It is a very serious threat. I have heard nothing here today that would make me feel any better about that.

Mr. Chairman, I will just express to you a personal story. I have had airline stewardesses come to me to talk to me about these big groups of Chinese that are riding at times when nobody is riding. I happened to see them on the airplane myself. Not just American Airlines but United Airlines.

They all looked like they just came out of a Goodwill store. They are dressed American and everything looks good. They don't say one word to each other because they have been told not to speak to one another because they are speaking in Chinese. They are going in groups and this doesn't look like a tourist group to me for some reason.

I would hope that somebody looks into that because I, too, have certainly passed on my observations to authorities. But no matter what we do to pass on our information, Mr. Chairman, if the system is broke, if we don't have—if the people on the front line and the law enforcement people don't have the backup of the American people, it is not going to work.

I would content that the reason the situation is broke is because there are economic and political factors in our country that don't want this system to function well and to work well. I would hope that what we are talking about today will open people's eyes to the fact of the relationship between this and the safety of our people in an era when there are terrorists who would destroy buildings in New York. Thank you very much, Mr. Chairman.

Mr. GALLEGLY. Thank you, Dana.

Mr. Royce.

Mr. ROYCE. Thank you. I wanted to ask a question of our panelists here going to the question of the culture at the Department of Homeland Security and the culture at the Department of State and whether or not things have really changed in terms of the issue that Congressman Rohrabacher just spoke to in terms of the issue of facilitating travel and trade over national security, if there hasn't been a change in the equilibrium. One of the observations I would make, if I could quote from an interview that Ms. Vaughan after 9/11.

You were a former consular official and you looked through those documents, that evidence that might have indicated that those 15 hijackers, at least that came out of Ryad, that they would have been disallowed. Joel Molbright wrote of that interview and he said that you said at the time the consular officers weren't asleep at the switch. The problem was that the supervisor's hands were over their eyes.

If we look at the details, we see that if the law had been enforced on the face of it, the 9/11 terrorists never would have entered the United States because most of them were young single men with no demonstrated means of support, with no ties to their home country, meaning they were classic overstay candidates. They would have been voted down on the issue of being classic overstay candidates. Yet, that is not what happened.

If we look at what did happen where we see that not only did this happen out of Ryad, but we had three additional terrorists who went through what is called Visa Express which started just 3 months before 9/11. Under that process, of course, that allowed Saudi Nationals and noncitizens alike to just submit their visa applications through their local Saudi travel agency. There wasn't even the opportunity to have a face-to-face.

The summation of this is a letter written to our Secretary of State Colin Powell by a colleague of mine who serves on our International Relations Committee with us. Congressman Burton wrote him and said,

> "At least one consular officer informed the General Accounting Office that she would not have granted the visas to some of the 9/11 hijackers that she granted these visas to if the State Department had had an informal policy that all Saudis—had not had an informal policy that all Saudis were presumed to be entitled to a visa."

Now, that stands the law on its head. So I guess the question goes back to the question of culture and whether that has changed and your perceptions on that.

The last question I wanted to ask you and leave you with, this new plan put forward as part of a worker program in the United States, in your view having had experience, Ms. Vaughan, in this area, will this make America less secure or more secure if the U.S. Congress were to ratify this proposal for a guess worker program. Mr. Nunez and the others, I would ask you the same question. Thank you very much.

Mr. GALLEGLY. Ms. Vaughan.

Ms. VAUGHAN. I have to say there is no question that the kind of massive so-called temporary guest worker program if enacted would make us less secure because there is simply no way that the agencies can manage the crush of applications that would result from such a program. It is just impossible.

To answer your first question, I would have to say, no. I don't believe the cultures have changed at either the State Department of the Department of Homeland Security and I think there is ample evidence and statements that have been made by officials to that effect.

Mr. NUNEZ. On the culture question I think the program—several of you have mentioned this. The problem starts at the top, not at the bottom. I think the border patrol on the line, the inspectors on duty, they want to do the right thing. The consular officials in the consulates would like to be able to do their job but they are told for good or bad by their superiors, "Don't do this," or, "Make the line move faster," or, "We are not going to patrol in this particular area."

You get a much different answer about what is happening in law enforcement if you talk to the political appointee or the leader as opposed to someone down at the working level. I think that the men and women of these agencies would love to be free to do their jobs the way you wrote the law. But, in many instances, and for many years they have been interfered with. Special interest, you know, and it is not just people in the White House or the Executive Branch.

I would imagine that many Congressmen get the opportunity to call some Government agency and say, "Why are you not doing what my constituent wants you to do?" The vadalia onion issue 4 or 5 years ago. I mean, certainly let us not go arrest somebody when they are in the middle of picking a crop. I mean, why not? They are here illegally.

I think I am proud to tell this story. Back when I was in the U.S. Attorney's Office some of you are aware of the race track down at Delmar. It is open from mid-July to mid-September. We sent the border patrol—this was before IRCA. We went the border patrol to the track about a week before the track season opened that year. They arrested probably, I don't know, 70, 80 percent of the people working in the stables who were taking care of the horses.

The millionaires who run this industry were outraged that they could see their lives flashing before their eyes. We said, "Fine. You don't want us to come back, you come up with some sort of a plan to make sure that you only hire U.S. citizens or legal people." It seems to me we have come a long way, unfortunately, from the time when we used to do things to remind the public that there is a law out there that needs to be obeyed.

We have done the opposite. We have sort of gone along with this notion that we are not going to care if you violate this law. It is the worst model for democracy to use. And then to try to convince newly emerging democracies adopt a rule of law and do like we do. Which part of the way we do this.

Mr. GALLEGLY. Thank you, Peter.

Mr. West.

Mr. WEST. On the culture issue, very quickly, I pretty much concur with what Mr. Nunez said, although I would say that in the ICE, in the Bureau of Immigration and Customs Enforcement, it is an agency that has combined U.S. Customs, Immigration and Investigations Division, Air Marshals, Detention and Removal Branch of INS. It is an agency that has so many missions and so many personnel now. The mission focus and the evolution incorporating all those people and functions, it is an agency that has got issues.

I would suggest that it has a lot of growing pains. On the issue of the pending guest worker/proposals having lived through and dealt with the 1986 legalization worker/employer sanctions program that was nothing but a monumental disaster, why in the work would the Congress want to take on a do something given the sheer numbers that are many, many more times greater. It would be nothing but a colossal disaster many times over. I can tell you it would be a huge, huge disaster for this country from my perspective.

Mr. GALLEGLY. Thank you, Mr. Royce.

Mr. Tancredo.

Mr. TANCREDO. Thank you, Mr. Chairman. I have been listening to this very interesting discussion here. I keep thinking about something that happened to me awhile back which maybe is a metaphor for our entire problem. That is, I was flying over the port of entry at Nogales and, of course, in Nogales, as everybody knows, it is about as flat as this table area. Nogales, Mexico/Nogales, Arizona port of entry. A line of cars maybe three miles long from Mexico trying to get into the United States. They are checking everything very carefully.

But as you fly in this helicopter, a mile and ½ or 2 miles on the other side of that border, people are coming across, driving their cars across into the desert. You can see them from the helicopter. Here we are, though, check, by God, at that port of entry very, very carefully. Much of our discussion here just makes me think about that incident.

I wish you could just respond to or give your impression of the effect of all of these sanctuary city laws, Los Angeles included. They are passing all these laws and saying essentially, “Look, if you are here illegally, no problem. We will not cooperate with the INS. We will not help out anybody. If we arrest someone for violation of a law here, we will not tell the INS about it.”

What is your impression of the effect of that kind of—that phenomena on national security issues? Also, beyond that, when we have people helping illegal aliens do their taxes and stuff like that.

Knowing it, you know. Working out ways so they can do their taxes and actually claim earned income tax credit. That is mostly what is happening. It is not to pay taxes.

Is that a violation of 1324? Does anybody think we should go after them for aiding and abetting? Even the city council people who do these kinds of things and say, "We will not help enforce the law of the land." What is your impression of the effect of those kinds of things on the national security interest? Starting with Ms. Vaughan.

Ms. VAUGHAN. Well, there is no question that the absence of interior enforcement completely undermines all we are trying to do at the border. I think most people would agree with that. With respect to having State and local law enforcement, that would be a tremendous force multiplier for our immigration service. I have never been able to understand why it is cooperation among law enforcement agencies at all levels is so difficult on this issue of immigration when we have no problem in extending it on other things.

For example, child support collection and things like that. It is very easy to get cooperation on things like that. We have never succeeded in doing it on immigration and it would be a tremendous help. Again, I think many of the rank and file law enforcement personnel would have no problem with it. It would just take leadership and acceptance of it.

Mr. GALLEGLY. Mr. Nunez.

Mr. NUNEZ. We used to do this. I mean, Jessica said we never succeeded. We haven't succeeded in the last 20 years. But before that it was routine for State and local law enforcement to cooperate with INS border patrol and all Federal officials. It was routine. Why does it happen? Because city councils and Mayors and boards of supervisors are pressured by local interest groups, mostly immigrant support groups, if you will, to leave us alone.

The word goes down from the Mayor or the city council to the Chief of Police "lay off" so they don't. They lay off. Intimidation. It is a disaster and I think beyond that. It becomes another magnet pulling here because if you are an illegal alien in Mexico or anywhere in the world you know,

> "I have to figure out some way to get there but I am pretty sure I will be able to get past the border patrol or the inspector.
>
> "After that, I am home free. I have nothing to worry about. Even if I get stopped by a cop, I am not going to be hassled. I will be able to live a life for as long as I want to live. I have a job. If I have a family, they will benefit from all of the free education and medical care . . ."

etc., etc., etc. I mean, how far—I mean, you talk about enticements.

Now, I believe that there was an effective interior enforcement strategy that included State and local Federal agencies. Some number of those illegal aliens would say,

> "It is not worth the risk because even if I get past the border, I know I am going to be in jeopardy of being arrested and deported. If I am deported, that goes on my record. I will never be able to come."

Mr. GALLEGLY. Thank you.

Mr. West.

Mr. WEST. Since 9/11 it should have been crystal clear that immigration issues are directly linked to national security issues. Pretty much that is the case, although there are immigration issues and then there are immigration issues. That is the problem.

You have immigration issues on the order of the 9/11 hijackers and terrorists that are illegal aliens. You have immigration issues that are dealing with the Mexican borders and the day laborers and the agricultural workers and the city councils that want to create sanctuaries and such.

Well, they are really all the same and that is the problem. Convincing people, the city councils and the Chiefs of Police and that sort of thing that they are the same is the problem. It all goes to politicizing this immigration law enforcement business that we alluded to before.

It does have a derogatory effect on literally national security issues because when you have those city councils telling the Chiefs of Police who tell their precinct captains and such, "Don't cooperate with the immigration law enforcers," then when they pick up the load of Mexicans in the van or something, that's one thing.

But when they stop a car that happens to have suspected perhaps illegal aliens that are perhaps Bali operatives who also cross the Mexican border and they don't call the immigration authorities because of that same policy, well, that is an issue.

Mr. GALLEGLY. Mr. Faleomavaega.

Mr. FALEOMAVAEGA. Thank you, Mr. Chairman. I want to complement Ms. Vaughan for her insights not only from her own personal experiences of the problems that we are having as far as visa applications are concerned. I know that from my own personal experience and some of my constituents, at least those who applied for visas, the consulate people themselves don't actually do the interviews. They let foreign nationals to be part of the process. A lot of times these foreign nationals don't really care when these people apply for the visas in a way that you really don't appreciate the whole operation.

I can understand where you are coming from and maybe we really need to have an overall on the whole process. But then you have also admitted that is something that the State Department really will have to define or do a little refinement in terms of separating the work of those who really are interested in doing visas as opposed to those in the long run who want to do political stuff. You also mentioned about with all the high tech things that we have, the human element sometimes is surely missing. Perhaps also that is something that we need to look at.

I wanted to ask you from your given experience do you really think that having the presence of air marshals would add security to our airline industry or would it cause more problems? I don't know if I am asking the right expert.

Ms. VAUGHAN. I would say that I think this concept of a layered defense with many different components so that you have safety nets in place to backstop failures at certain other layers is very, very important. That is why despite the fact that the visa process cannot hope to catch every terrorist, it still is important that we have an efficient and effective system.

Mr. FALEOMAVAEGA. That is a very creative idea of having air marshals and also have pilots to be armed. That is another—is that an added feature that will add security or cause us more problems?

Ms. VAUGHAN. That is a question for you folks to decide. I really don't have any opinion on that issue.

Mr. FALEOMAVAEGA. I want to ask Mr. Nunez, you expressed concern about the waiver visa program. I am familiar with State of Hawaii whose entire economy depends on tourism. Of course, without the Japanese service, you have a real serious situation there in one of our States. Do you think that the waiver visa probably needs overhauling or is there some problems with it do you see, or is it pretty good the way it is being implemented?

Mr. NUNEZ. No, I don't think it is correct the way it is now. That is not to say that there might not be some way to revise it or to improve it so that at least there is some way to expedite some people from some countries. I am reasonably sure we could do that. But the way it is not is just sort of a blanket waiver for that country. Anybody in that country essentially can take advantage of it.

I think the questions earlier point out that, you know, whether it is Germany or France or Britain or whatever country, I mean, there is no reason to believe that every one of those citizens of those countries is somebody we would want to be involved in the waiver program. It seems to me we should try to fix it if possible. If we can't fix it, end it but don't keep it the way it is.

Mr. FALEOMAVAEGA. I would like to ask Mr. West in terms of your concerns about the border situation between us and Mexico and the idea that we try to establish a wall. I wanted to ask your thoughts on that. I know it is a very controversial issue for some of us and wanted to know if it is justified and we should build a wall between Mexico and our country. I suppose if Israel can do it, why can't we?

Mr. TANCREDO. Make good neighbors.

Mr. WEST. I assume you mean there is a fence—I am not from California so there is a short section of fence that is on the California side of the border down here?

Mr. FALEOMAVAEGA. You can call it a fence but I consider it a wall.

Mr. GALLEGLY. It is both.

Mr. WEST. It is my understanding that in the areas of the border where there has been a fence erected that it has been pretty readily compromised. Unless the Government is willing to erect a structure that is pretty much impenetrable, and I don't see that happening, it seems to be probably a waste of effort because people will find a way to get around it or through it. Unless we are willing to go all the way with it and if there is a political will to do that, that is one thing, but if you are going to take half measures that people on the other side are going to get around or over, what is the point?

Mr. NUNEZ. Can I add to that because I am from San Diego and I have been there before and after the fence. I can tell you that, whatever you want to call it, there actually is a fence of metal and then there is behind it a concrete fence they call it. For the people that live on the U.S. side of the border, it is a night and day difference. If you ask them, "Should we take the fence down?" they would lynch you because for them their quality of life has gone up tremendously.

The number of apprehensions in San Diego were over half a million a year until they built the fence, but the lights in, and put some more border patrol out there. Now it is less than 100,000. The traffic has shifted to places where there is no fence. Maybe we need to build more fences somewhere else but let us not take down the fences in the areas where it has worked.

Mr. GALLEGLY. Thank you very much. We have kind of gone just a little past our invitation but I would yield for the purposes of closing statement or closing question, 30 seconds, to my friend, the Ranking Member, Mr. Sherman.

Mr. SHERMAN. The rule of law works when we agree what the law should be, we write it clearly, and we enforce it. There is, unfortunately, in this country no agreement on what our real immigration law—not the text but the real immigration law should be. A major part of that disagreement is Americans want jobs that pay $10, $15, $20 an hour.

Employers don't want to pay $10 an hour. They define a job as one no American would take as a job they don't want to pay $10 an hour to do. Therefore, they decide that we need to import workers while, of course, in other ways, we are exporting jobs. Needless to say, our internal disagreement on what our laws should be with regard to economic immigration is exploited by terrorists because the vast majority of people crossing our borders are doing so as tourist or as economic immigrants and it is very easy in this shadow land where we don't know what the law is in terms of what we are really willing to enforce terrorist have been able to exploit.

I would hope that our friends in the Judiciary Committee and elsewhere would device a system that we can all get behind and then enforce instead of this cognitive dissidence that we have.

Mr. GALLEGLY. Thank you, gentlemen, Ranking Member. I would just like to close by associating myself directly with a comment that Mr. Nunez made and others relative to interior enforcement. Make no mistake about it, the overwhelming majority of those that are coming to the United States illegally are coming for economic purposes. The majority are not terrorists. There is a small—very small but very critical percentage that do have other intentions, to harm America.

I firmly believe if we went back to the law of the 1986 bill about interior enforcement which we did not do, it seems coincidental that Mr. Nunez mentioned 20 years ago we had enforcement but since IRCA we have not. If we eliminated access to jobs, access to benefits, then we would not need an inordinate number of border patrol to remove the—to take the people back home.

They would go on their own and they would not come here. I firmly believe that is the single most significant way that we can eliminate the illegal immigration population. What illegal immigration population we would have left would be the ones that we could really focus on, the bad guys, the potential terrorists and so on and so forth. That is an editorial comment that I have very strong feelings about.

I would like to ask just one last question. I think it kind of summarizes where we have been today of Mr. West. Has the management culture of the Department of Homeland Security and the Department of State really changed or is it still a priority of facilitating travel and trade over counterterrorism?

Mr. WEST. I believe within the Department of Homeland Security it has changed but it is a work in progress within the Department of State. I think in the working rank and file levels I would like to—I can't say that it has. I believe the culture there always has been and probably still is their job is to facilitate travel so, unfortunately, that is my perspective on that.

Mr. GALLEGLY. Thank you for your candor, Mr. West.

Ms. Sterling, thank you for making the trek from Dallas. Mr. Nunez, it is always an honor to have you with us. Ms. Vaughan, thank you very much.

Thanks to my colleagues, Eni Faleomavaega for making the trek out, Tom Tancredo from Colorado, and my good friend and neighbor from the valley, Brad Sherman, Dana Rohrabacher, and Ed Royce. Thank you all. The meeting stands adjourned.

[Whereupon, at 12:25 p.m. the meeting was adjourned.]

APPENDIX

Material Submitted for the Hearing Record

Letters of Response to Questions Asked During the Hearing

American Airlines

Peggy Sterling
Vice President
Safety, Security & Environmental

June 1, 2004

The Honorable Elton Gallegly
253 Ford House Office Building
Washington, DC 20515

Dear Mr. Chairman:

In response to your question regarding "last minute" ticket sales, American Airlines does in fact provide one-way group ticket inventory on flights departing from Los Angeles, CA to Chicago O'Hare, Boston, Washington Dulles, Newark, NJ, and JFK. An agency or ticket planner, not an individual customer, can purchase discount tickets in advance up to three hours before departure. However, passenger names must be provided when tickets are booked so names can be processed in the computer-assisted passenger prescreening system (CAPPS) as outlined in TSA Aviation Security Directive 1544-01-10X – Section I. paragraph E.

In regards to passenger acceptance, American Airlines strictly adheres to passenger identity check directives as outlined in Section VII, D of the Aircraft Operator Standard Security Program (AOSSP). Passengers checking baggage must present a valid ID at the time of check-in and when they proceed through airport security checkpoints. If the ID presented contains an expiration date, carrier representatives verify that the ID has not expired. Acceptable forms of ID include:

1. A photo ID issued by a government authority

2. Two other forms of ID, at least one of which shall be issued by a government authority, or

3. An air carrier issued photo ID, when the passenger is a direct air carrier employee of the air carrier providing transport.

If the passenger cannot provide proper identification, he/she shall be designated a "selectee" passenger. This designation requires that passengers undergo additional screening on their bags and person. Baggage screening could include Explosive Detection Systems (EDS), Explosive Trace Detection (ETD) screening and/or physical search.

Mr. Gallegly, if I can be of further assistance, please do not hesitate to let me know.

Respectfully,

Peggy E. Sterling

Peggy Sterling
American Airlines
Vice President -
Safety, Security & Environmental

U.S. Department of Justice

Federal Bureau of Investigation

Washington, D. C. 20535-0001

March 1, 2004

Honorable Elton Gallegly
Chairman
Subcommittee on International Terrorism, Nonproliferation
and Human Rights
Committee on International Relations
United States House of Representatives
Washington, D.C. 20515

Dear Mr. Chairman:

During the February 13, 2004 hearing in Los Angeles before the Subcommittee on International Terrorism, Nonproliferation and Human Rights, Congressman Sherman asked whether the transliteration of foreign names could be accomplished uniformly and consistently throughout the United States government so that searches for this information would not miss "matches" merely because of different spellings. FBI Deputy Assistant Director Bob Garrity promised to obtain a response to this question.

Section 352 of the Intelligence Authorization Act of 2003 directed the intelligence community (IC) to develop "a standardized method for transliterating into the Roman alphabet personal and place names originally rendered in any language that uses an alphabet other than the Roman alphabet."

In compliance with this instruction, the Assistant Director of Central Intelligence for Analysis and Production assembled language experts from throughout the IC, including FBI experts, to develop a standardized system for the transliteration of Arabic names. This system was reviewed and approved by the National Intelligence Analysis and Production Board and distributed to the IC in June 2003. Similarly, standards for the transliteration of Hindi and Urdu names were promulgated in November 2003, and linguists are now working on transliteration standards for Persian-Farsi and for Dari, which will be finalized this spring. Standards will follow for other key languages, including Korean and Russian.

The FBI has had a longstanding interest in standardizing the transliteration of names, and in the summer of 2002 began training all FBI personnel who work with foreign names in using the predecessors to the recent standards. The FBI has trained nearly 500 employees in transliterating Arabic names, introduced a course in Chinese transliteration in the spring of 2003, and will continue to work to ensure that all linguists are instructed in the IC standards as they are adopted.

I hope this information is helpful. If I can be of further assistance, please do not hesitate to contact me or my staff at (202) 324-4510.

Sincerely,

Eleni P. Kalisch
Assistant Director
Office of Congressional Affairs

1 - Honorable Brad Sherman
Ranking Member
Subcommittee on International Terrorism, Nonproliferation and Human Rights
Committee on International Relations
United States House of Representatives
Washington, D.C. 20515